LAFOSSE & ALEXANDER'S
Origami
Jewelry

TUTTLE Publishing

Tokyo | Rutland, Vermont | Singapore

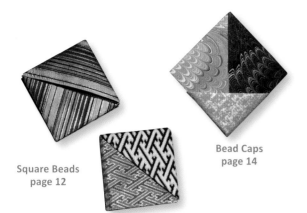

Square Beads
page 12

Bead Caps
page 14

Pillow Beads
page 18

Square Rhombus
Beads
page 20

Arrowhead Beads
page 41

Contents

Slinking Triangle
Beads
page 58

Angel Wings
page 54

Abstract Sail
Elements
page 51

Wolverine Claws
page 49

Trident Beads
page 47

Preliminary Form
Connectors
page 23

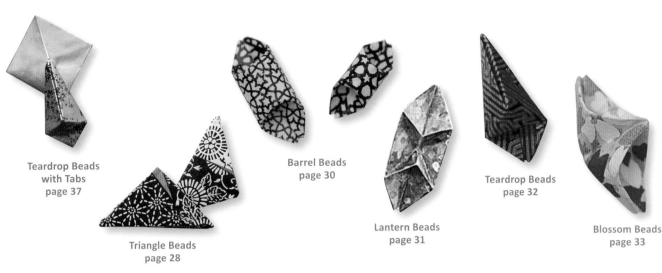

Teardrop Beads
with Tabs
page 37

Triangle Beads
page 28

Barrel Beads
page 30

Lantern Beads
page 31

Teardrop Beads
page 32

Blossom Beads
page 33

Twin Arrowhead
Beads
page 44

Owl Beads
page 43

Duo Kite Beads
page 45

Preliminary Form
Beads
page 39

Lantern Beads
with Tabs
page 37

Barrel Beads
with Tabs
page 36

The Origamido Studio

Some of the most popular purchases from the Origamido Studio are stunning pieces of origami jewelry. We fold many, but not most, of the pieces we sell. Artist friends and students, after being inspired at a class, or by one of our designs, often bring their expertly crafted paper jewelry to display proudly for purchase in our showcase.

The Origamido shops in Boston, Massachusetts and Hawai'i.

Our jewelry customers return often, bringing family members or friends to see what's new in the case. They are often wearing pieces from earlier visits, but sometimes sporting new pieces of their own design.

We wrote this book for the jewelry-making novice and expert alike. Anyone hoping to incorporate beautiful papers and other foldable materials into their wearable creations using origami techniques will be pleased to find that the origami elements in

Origamido Studio's jewelry on display.

this book do not require you to be an origami expert. Nor do you need to be expert at reading origami diagrams, because the accompanying DVD video contains exclusive lessons that demonstrate the folding methods for all of our various origami beads and elements. Diagrams are provided for those who enjoy their convenience, and for beginners who want to better understand other books by learning this handy international "origami shorthand."

Origami jewelry can and should be celebrated, not feared, and so this book addresses concerns for paper quality and for the robustness of design. In this book and DVD set, we discuss selecting the best papers, preparing them (by laminating or back-coating), and wet-folding them with paste (for adding the necessary body and strength). We have also designed several new, versatile, folded "jewels." You will love arranging and combining these elements with other materials such as seashells, or beads of glass, metal, plastic, or stone. By using readily available findings and fittings you will create attractive, wonderfully expressive and distinctive, wearable folded jewelry art. People notice and comment about origami jewelry because it is so unusual. Origami jewelry is a natural conversation starter. Friends will ask, "Did you fold your earrings?" Now you can say, "Yes, of course!"

Origami Symbols Key

The origami diagrams used in this book are an efficient, internationally-standardized system of lines and arrows, dots, dashes, and a few other symbols.

Although simple, it is not immediately intuitive, so please invest a few moments to study the key, and refer back to it as needed. Become familiar with the symbols and what they mean. As you watch the DVD, look at the corresponding diagrams in the book to reinforce your understanding. For efficiency, a diagram may contain more than one instruction, so check carefully for details you might have overlooked at first. If you are unsure of a step, glancing ahead to the next step often reveals the desired shape, and may provide other valuable clues. Rotate the paper for your comfort as you fold it (even though the diagrams will not show the object rotated), and then return it to the position shown in the diagram as you compare the shapes. Once you learn this elegant diagramming system, you will be able to enjoy countless origami books.

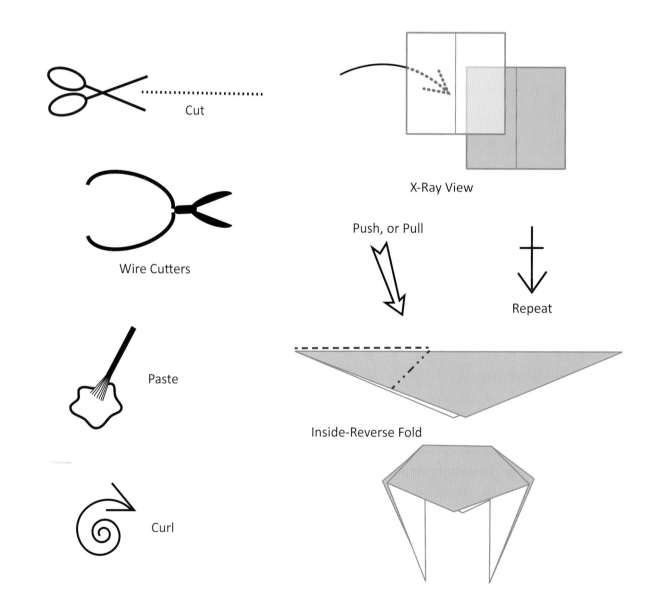

Cut

Wire Cutters

Paste

Curl

X-Ray View

Push, or Pull

Repeat

Inside-Reverse Fold

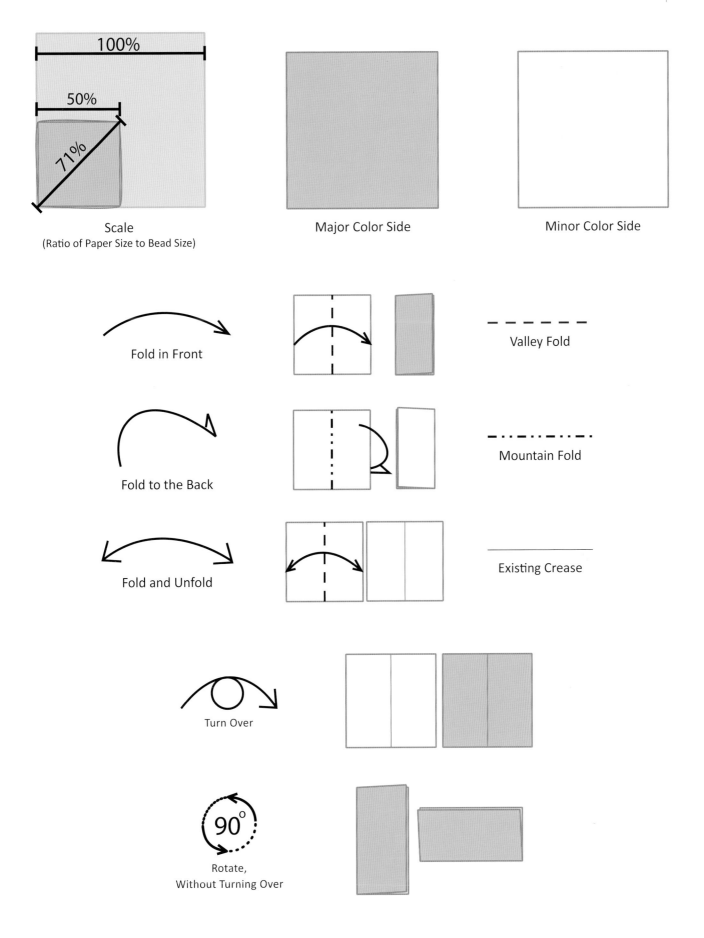

Scale
(Ratio of Paper Size to Bead Size)

100%

50%

71%

Major Color Side

Minor Color Side

Fold in Front

Valley Fold

Fold to the Back

Mountain Fold

Fold and Unfold

Existing Crease

Turn Over

90°

Rotate,
Without Turning Over

Our Origamido Jewelry Design System

Good design is most often simple, and so we begin by exploring the wealth of possibilities within the most simple and familiar bases.

All origami objects are abstract by virtue of the folding process. It is this abstraction of an idea into geometric planes, shadows, and angles that provides origami jewelry with the potential for achieving a unique and timeless elegance. Just as the crystalline structures of gemstones and the architectural windings of seashells have enchanted humans for longer than anyone can know, origami's geometric underpinnings make it so inviting to the eye, intriguing to the mind, and entrancing to the spirit.

We often use the musical performance as a teaching analogy for folded art. Well-chosen paper is the instrument. If the paper is patterned, the scale of the patterns, colors, and textures will provide tone, and even play their own notes, too. The design is like the musical composition that provides the strength and substance necessary for durability. Elegant results demand a careful, heartfelt execution, or a cogent interpretation during your performance. Refining your folding skills takes "practice, practice, practice" as does playing any musical instrument artfully.

Beginning with the preliminary form—four sets of alternating mountain and valley creases radiating from the center of the square—numerous different, elegant, and durable "beads" result from varying just a few subsequent folds. These sturdy elements can be simply strung and hung as necklace pendants or earrings, or combined by tabbing and tiling. Most of our origami jewelry elements are folded from single squares such as these, but multi-piece, interlocking designs (connected with tabs and pockets) are particularly useful for making interesting cluster arrangements, or adjustable-length necklaces, bracelets, belts, and bands.

Left: Fancy papers make excellent jewelry after laminating (back-coating with paste) for adding body and strength.

Right: Back-coated florist's foils make versatile folded "beads."

Wearability is Critical

Durability and comfort are the greatest concerns expressed by potential customers. Few materials available to the jeweler are as amazingly varied as paper.

Origami jewelry components are lightweight. Nevertheless, fancy papers, especially the most beautiful, are usually too soft for jewelry use, and so we recommend reinforcement by pasting them to a stronger material. Adding this extra layer with paste is called "back-coating" and it provides added body to otherwise flimsy papers.

Durability and comfort are not just about the materials, but also about the design of the piece. For example, our necklaces often have stone, plastic, glass, or metal elements placed around the back of the neck to ensure comfort where the necklace hugs the skin. Good design should allow the paper elements to be pretty up front, while letting the more durable materials do the job they do best.

Finally, the folded elements do not exist without support, and there is a huge variety of fittings, findings, and adhesives that integrate the components. Take care when attaching, stringing, mounting or connecting your painstakingly folded elements, and use the highest quality materials that you can afford.

Folded, multi-layer pasted paper "jewels" can be used with most conventional jewelry-making materials. Shown above left: Single Barrel paper "beads" held between chains with crimped, metal jingle-bells. Right: Triple Barrel paper "beads" on a glass bead necklace.

Origami "Jewels"

As Earrings...

page 14

page 23

page 28

page 37

page 43

page 58

page 36

page 49

page 51

...and as Necklaces!

page 14

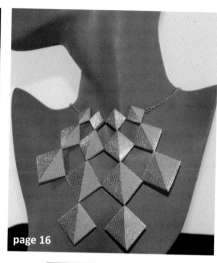

page 16

page 20

page 45

page 41

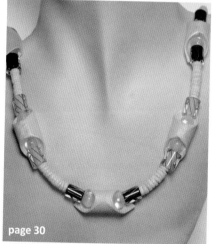

page 30

page 33

page 32

page 49

Square Beads

*Designed by Michael G. LaFosse
from a traditional base*

The Square Bead is easy to fold, quick to make, and it displays the paper's features beautifully. This bead is the real workhorse of our origami jewelry design system, and we use it time and again. Combining various sizes of Square Beads with other elements provides endless possibilities for distinctive folded jewelry. This bead consists of two squares, each folded to the "upside-down sailboat" shape (step 5) used throughout this book.

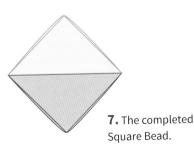

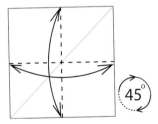

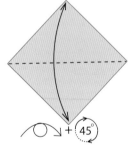

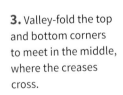

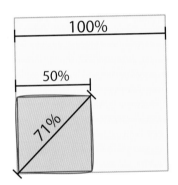

1. Begin with the display side up. Valley-fold in half, bottom corner to top. Unfold. Turn over and rotate 45 degrees.

2. Valley-fold in half, edge to edge, both ways, unfolding after each. Rotate 45 degrees.

3. Valley-fold the top and bottom corners to meet in the middle, where the creases cross.

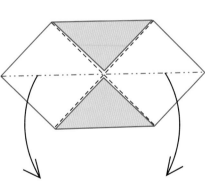

4. Use the existing mountain and valley creases to collapse the model, folding the left and right corners in half and moving them to meet at the bottom.

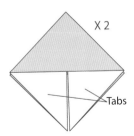

5. Your paper should look like this. You will need two units of the same size for each square bead.

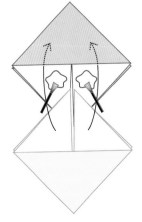

6. Apply paste to the top surface of the two sail-shaped tabs of one unit. Slide the two units together with the paste in-between the tabs of both units.

7. The completed Square Bead.

Methods for Mounting Square Beads

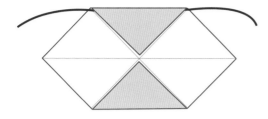

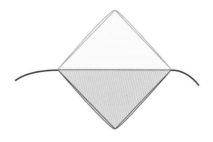

1. Insert the beading string or a suitable wire space-holder at step 4 on page 12. This may be done to one or both units. (A double strand is more secure and may help to prevent twisting of the beads while wearing.)

2. Square Bead on string. The result of this method is that the dividing line between the two units will be in line with the string.

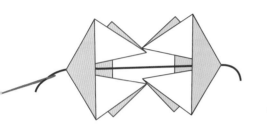

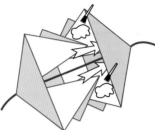

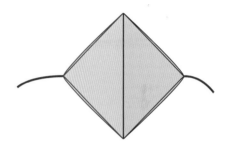

1. Alternately, the Square Bead units may be strung with a needle and cord, piercing the folded corner at what was once the center of the square sheet.

2. Apply paste to the tabs just before sliding the units together.

3. The result of this method is that the dividing line between the two units will be perpendicular to the string.

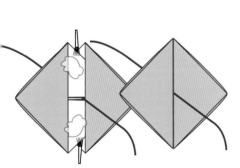

Yet another way to string Square Beads is through the center, perpendicular to the face. There will be a natural space available for use just before the two units are fully joined.

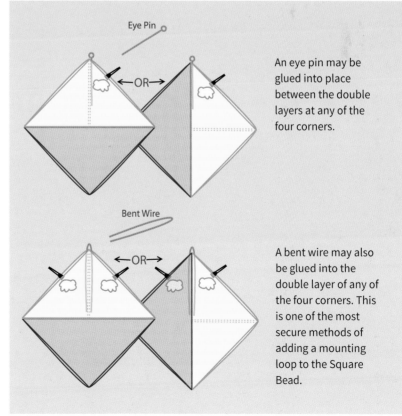

Eye Pin

←OR→

An eye pin may be glued into place between the double layers at any of the four corners.

Bent Wire

←OR→

A bent wire may also be glued into the double layer of any of the four corners. This is one of the most secure methods of adding a mounting loop to the Square Bead.

Bead Caps

*Designed by Michael G. LaFosse
from traditional bases*

Bead Caps are used for decorative contrast, setting an additional right triangle perpendicular to those two displayed in the Square Bead. It may also serve to secure one or two corners of a Square Bead for mounting purposes, and to add more colors and shapes to a piece of jewelry consisting of several Square Beads.

Here we present several styles of Bead Caps: Triangle, Square, Pentagon, and Fiesta (see facing page). You may develop more variations on your own; experimenting with different sizes of Bead Caps will alter the look. Thinner papers usually produce the best looking Bead Caps.

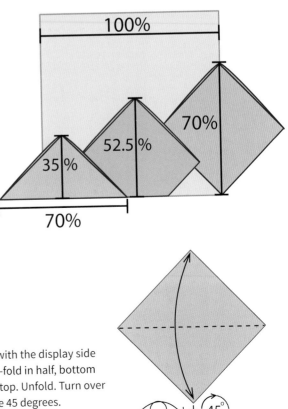

1. Begin with the display side up. Valley-fold in half, bottom corner to top. Unfold. Turn over and rotate 45 degrees.

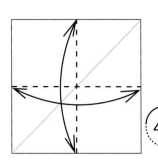

2. Valley-fold in half, edge to edge both ways, unfolding after each. Rotate 45 degrees.

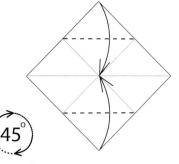

3. Valley-fold the top and bottom corners to meet at the center, where the creases intersect.

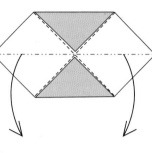

4. Use the existing creases to collapse the form, moving the left and right corners to the bottom.

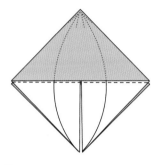

5. Valley-fold the bottom corners up, tucking them inside the paper, forming two triangle-shaped interior tabs.

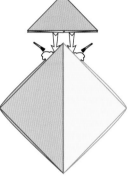

6. Fit one corner of a Square Bead into the Bead Cap. Use the two interior tabs of the Bead Cap to align the pieces, fitting them into the corner pockets of the Square Bead. Use a little glue or paste to secure the cap permanently.

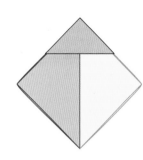

7. The completed Triangle Bead Cap on a Square Bead.

Bead Cap Variations

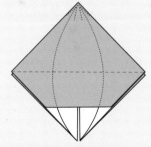

Here is the **Pentagon** Bead Cap (see the folding method described in the sidebar). See page 26 for a Fish-Shaped Bead that showcases this cap.

Square Bead Cap: Omit the corner folds at step 3, and then proceeding to collapse the shape and fold the two tabs inside. Attach as in step 6.

Fan-folding the free corner of a Square Bead Cap makes a lovely triangle pattern, called "**Fiesta**." This is especially effective when using paper that is colored differently on each side.

Pentagon Bead Cap

1. Fold Triangle Bead Cap steps 1 and 2; at step 3, fold the top and bottom corners only to the level indicated by the crease-ends, marked by the "X" arrowhead in the diagram.

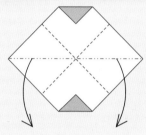

2. Use the existing creases to collapse the form, moving the left and right corners to the bottom.

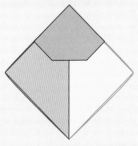

3. Valley-fold the bottom corners up, tucking them inside the paper, forming two triangle-shaped interior tabs.

4. The completed Pentagon Bead Cap, attached to a square bead using the method demonstrated in step 6.

Square Bead Mounting Covers

Designed by Michael G. LaFosse from traditional bases

A blintzed square is attached to the outside of a Square Bead. It may be calculated to cover the Square Bead exactly or it may be folded from larger paper that will solidly frame a Square Bead. Structurally, Square Beads are sturdier with Mounting Covers, and the covers provide a handy way to conceal a wire or a string. Mounting Covers allow you to feature a design or pattern of the paper without interrupting creases. They also help secure the other two halves of the Square Bead.

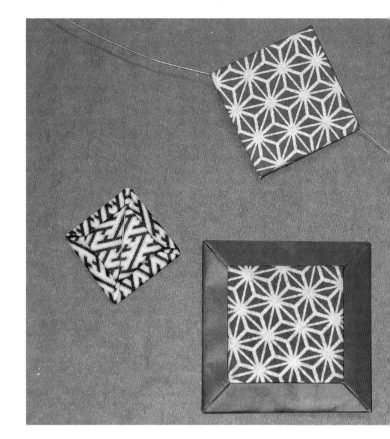

Basic Square Bead Cover: The cover is calculated to fit the size of a Square Bead exactly; one or both sides of the Square Bead may be covered. The decorative effect of this cover is to make a clean tile out of the Square Bead, without the diagonal delineation. Functionally, this cover makes tiled arrays of Square Beads look clean and elegant by canceling the wirework.

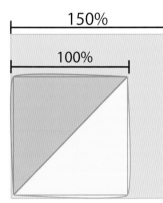

1. Measure the length of the Square Bead you wish to cover, and then trim the square cover paper to be 1½ times as long.

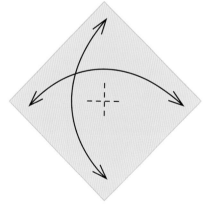

2. Beginning with the non-display side up, valley-fold in half diagonally both ways, unfolding after each. Make only short creases, just enough to mark the center of the square.

3. Valley-fold each of the four corners to the center where the creases cross. Unfold.

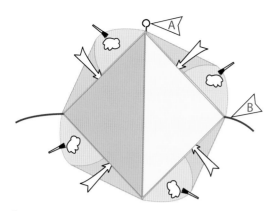

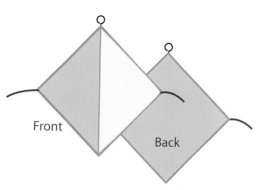

4. Apply paste to the inside of each of the four triangular flaps of the framing paper. Tuck each of the four corners into the open pockets at the edges of the Square Bead. Notice that you could paste an eye pin (A) or insert a stringing cord (B).

5. The completed single Square Bead Mounting Cover, front and back. You could also apply a second cover to the other side.

Tile Bib Necklace

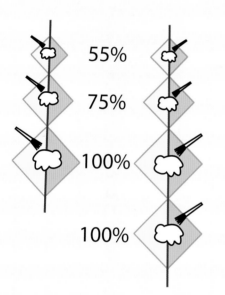

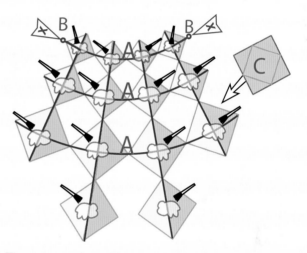

6. Make two strands each of graduated sizes of Square Beads, connect diagonally using beading wire and glue.

7. Arrange the strands as shown. (A) Paste the horizontal cords in place. Let dry completely. (B) Paste an eye pin on each of the two top, outermost squares, indicated with an "X" arrowhead. (C) Apply a Mounting Cover to the back of each Square Bead. Let dry completely.

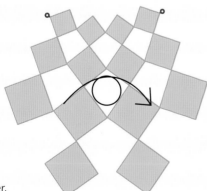

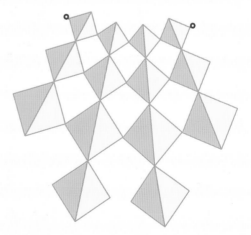

8. Turn over.

9. The completed tiled Bib with eye pins, ready for mounting to a neck chain.

Pillow Beads

*Designed by Michael G. LaFosse
from traditional bases*

Why not take advantage of the four edge slits in your Square Bead to create a sturdy and attractive frame? In origami, the term *blintz* refers to folding four corners to meet at the center. A double blintz creates more layers, making the assembly even more substantial. Simply by "double-blintzing" a third square of paper, we can form tabs on the third piece that can each be inserted into corresponding slits of the Square Bead. One useful feature of this geometry is that every double blintz fits every smaller Square Bead. We call the combination a Pillow Bead, because it reminds us of Grandma's fancy pillows with an extending edge of fringe or lace, forming a contrasting and attractive border.

The double blintz makes a sturdy frame with no cut edges of paper showing. Each time you blintz a square, the area is cut in half, so the size of the paper necessary for a double-blintzed frame for your square bead must be at least three times the area of the paper you folded for the Square Bead, but that could make a tight fit. Use an initial square that is 3½ times the height of the Square Bead to ensure that it will be completely covered. A 1-inch (2.5-cm) Square Bead requires a 3½-inch (9-cm) square of paper. Of course, larger frames are possible, too. Experiment with different proportions to determine which best serves your needs.

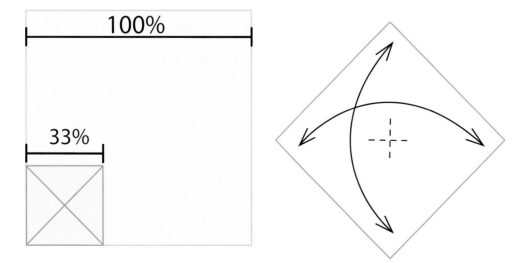

1. Begin with a square that is 3½ times taller than the measure of the Square Bead you wish to frame. Beginning with the non-display side up, valley-fold in half diagonally both ways, unfolding after each. Make only short creases, just enough to mark the center of the square.

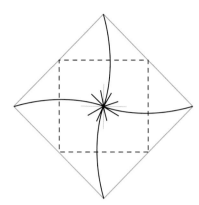

2. Valley-fold each of the four corners to the center where the creases cross.

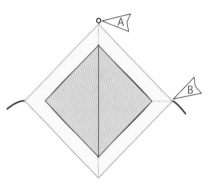

3. Valley-fold each of the four new corners to the center, and then unfold to return each to their original position.

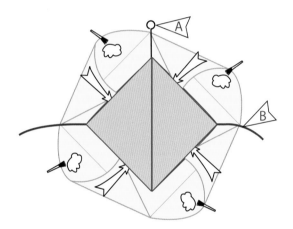

4. Apply paste to the inside of each of the four triangle flaps of the framing paper. Tuck each of the four corners into the open pockets at the edges of the Square Bead. Notice that you could paste an eye pin (A) or insert a stringing cord (B).

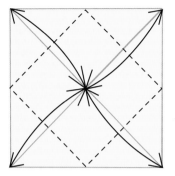

5. The completed Pillow Bead, showing both optional mounts.

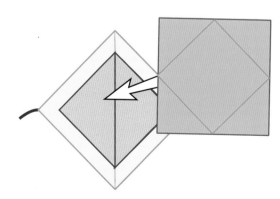

6. You may apply a Square Bead Mounting Cover, displaying an undivided square area of contrasting or decorative material.

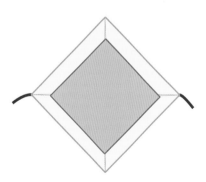

7. The Pillow Bead with a cover.

Square Rhombus Beads

Designed by Michael G. LaFosse from traditional bases

This bead takes advantage of the triangular flap normally hidden inside. The flaps may also be covered by folding a separate piece called the Rhombus Base (see page 27). Folding these flaps to the outside provides new decorative and structural options. You will surely discover many variations not shown in this book. Consider using paper colored differently on both sides if you will not be adding the folded Rhombus Cover, but using paper colored the same on both sides is fine.

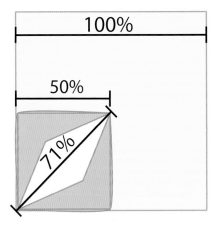

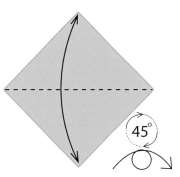

1. Begin with the display side of the paper facing up. Valley-fold in half, bottom corner to top. Unfold. Turn over and rotate 45 degrees.

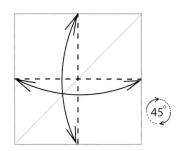

2. Valley-fold in half both ways, edge to edge, unfolding after each. Rotate 45 degrees so that the diagonal crease is horizontal.

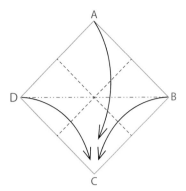

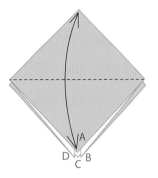

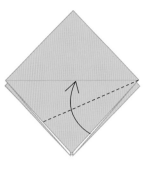

3. Use the existing mountain and valley creases to collapse the form, moving each of the four corners to meet at the bottom.

4. Valley-fold corner "A" to the top and return it to the bottom.

5. Valley-fold the bottom right edge of the top layer to the crease.

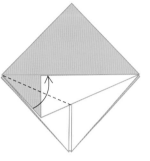

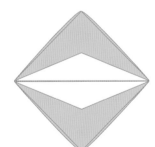

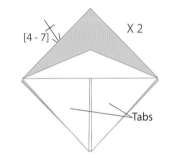

6. Valley-fold the bottom left edge of the top layer to the crease.

7. Valley-fold the resulting triangular flap up.

8. Repeat steps 4 through 7 on the other side. Prepare a second unit.

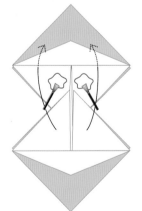

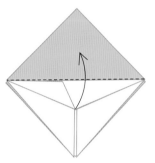

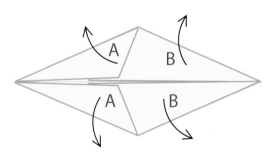

9. Apply paste to the top surface of the two sail-shaped tabs of one unit. Slide the two units together with the paste in-between the tabs of both units.

10. The completed Square Rhombus Bead. You will notice the split rhombus shape across the middle. This may be left as is, or it may be covered with a Rhombus Cover in complimentary paper, as shown in steps 11–16. You may use the same stringing and mounting methods as for the Square Bead, described on page 13.

11. Use a Rhombus Base (page 27) folded from a square the same size as your Square Rhombus Bead for a decorative cover. Unfold the "A" flaps first, then the "B" flaps of the Rhombus Base.

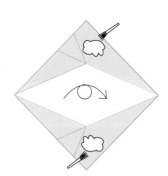

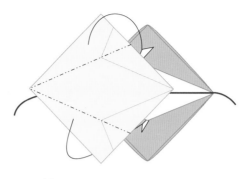

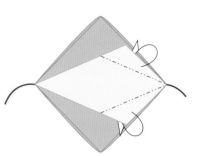

12. Apply paste to the areas highlighted in blue. Turn over to apply the glued side to the bead.

13. Mountain-fold the full-length flaps first, wrapping them around the back of the flaps on the bead. Carefully center the shape. Consider positioning your stringing cord at this time, or you may use a needle and cord to string beads at a later time.

14. Mountain-fold to wrap the remaining two flaps.

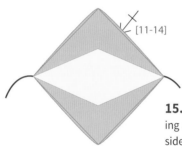

[11-14]

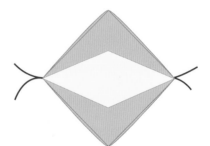

15. Prepare another covering and apply it to the other side of the bead.

16. The covered Square Rhombus Bead. Notice that a stringing cord has been passed through both sides, front and back. This is most secure and stable, and keeps the beads aligned more easily when they are worn. Single covered Square Rhombus Beads may also be mounted using eye pins or even a bent piece of wire, as shown in the Square Bead project on page 13.

Preliminary Form Connectors

The preliminary form is a classic origami base that is used to begin many thousands of folded paper designs. We use Preliminary Form Connectors (PFCs) in our origami jewelry system as a connecting device; there are four distinct forms: Square Front and Back; Kite Front/Square Back; Kite Front and Back; and Opposed Kites.

The Square Front and Back is used to connect Square Beads to Square Beads. Its square corners provide a perfect fit. A Kite Front/Square Back unit connects one acute corner of a Rhombus to the square corner of a Square Bead: The narrow corner of the kite measures 45 degrees, which matches an acute corner of the Rhombus. By folding the Rhombus in half and adding another Kite Front/Square Back, we can form an isosceles triangle loop for hanging. We use the Kite Front/Square Back to connect the two acute corners of a Rhombus after being folded in half, forming an isosceles triangle loop.

The diagonal height of the connector is the most useful measure for design consideration, as the visual scale below indicates. Connectors of varying sizes may be used depending upon the desired proportions of the design. Although the connectors will be invisible in the final piece, the length of the lock they provide is significant: the larger the connector the more overlap between joined pieces.

Glue need not be used during the design and fitting stages, but it should be used at final assembly for permanent results.

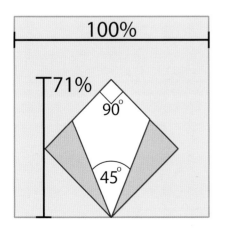

Square Front/Square Back PFC

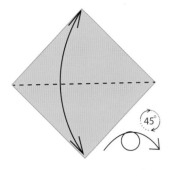

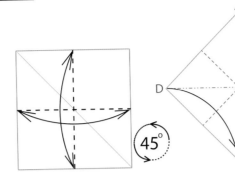

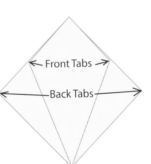

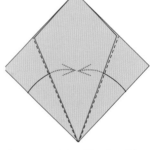

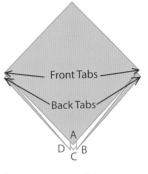

1. Begin display side up. Valley-fold in half diagonally, bottom corner to top. Unfold. Turn over and rotate 45 degrees.

2. Valley-fold in half, edge to edge, both ways, unfolding after each. Rotate 45 degrees.

3. Use the existing creases to collapse the form, moving the four corners to the bottom.

4. The completed Square Front/Square Back Preliminary Form Connector. Note the identification of the front and back tab sets.

Kite Front/Square Back PFC

Open Edges

1. Mountain-fold the bottom, open edges of the front tab set, forming a kite shape on the front of the connector.

2. The completed Kite Front/Square Back Preliminary Form Connector. Note the identification of the front and back tab sets.

Kite Front and Back PFC

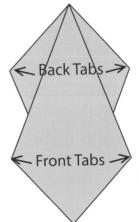

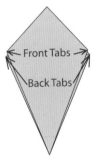

1. Begin with a Kite Front/Square Back PFC shown to the left, with the wide end of the kite positioned at the top. Valley-fold the bottom left and right edges of the square in to the center, behind the front kite.

2. The completed Kite Front and Back Preliminary Form Connector. Note the identification of the front and back tab sets.

Opposed Kites PFC

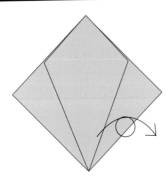

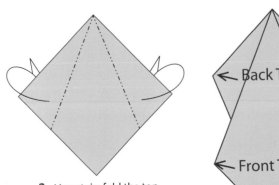

1. Begin with a Kite Front/Square Back PFC (above) with the wide end of the kite positioned at the top. Turn over, left to right.

2. Mountain-fold the top left and right edges of the square to the hidden vertical inside folds.

3. The completed Opposed Kites PFC. Note the identification of the front and back tab sets.

Connecting Two Square Beads with a PFC

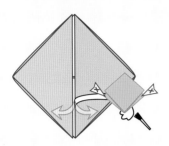

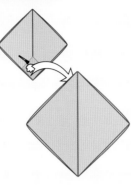

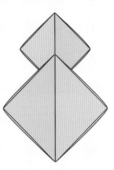

1. Apply glue to one side of the connector and insert it, glue side in, behind the slot on the front side of a Square Bead. Slide the connector into the bottom corner of the Square Bead and close the bead tightly.

2. Apply glue to the front side of the connector and fit its tabs into the back slot of another Square Bead, positioning and closing the new bead as desired.

3. Two Square Beads connected. You may connect many square beads in this way and use the same or different sizes. Chains of connected beads can be made into hoops for bracelets.

Pendant Mount

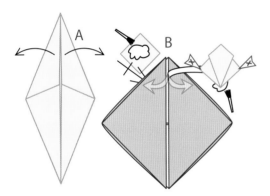

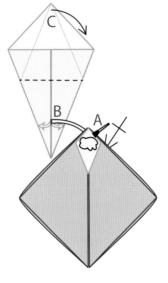

1. You can use two Kite Front/Square Back Preliminary Form Connectors to attach a Rhombus Base (page 27) for a pendant mount. (A) Have ready a Rhombus Base, folded to any desired size for the design, and unfold the top flaps. (B) Apply glue to the square sides of the two Kite Front/Square Back Preliminary Form Connectors. Insert these two connectors—one in front and one in back—into the top slotted corner of a Square Bead, kites exposed.

2. (A) Apply glue to the kites of the connectors. (B) Insert the kite of one side into the bottom acute corner slot of the partially opened Rhombus Bead. (C) Valley-fold the top half of the Rhombus Base down in front of the Square Bead.

3. Mountain-fold the open flaps of the Rhombus Base behind the layers of the kite side of the connector, trapping it.

4. The completed Square Bead with Rhombus Base Pendant Mount.

Other Preliminary Form Connector Usage Ideas

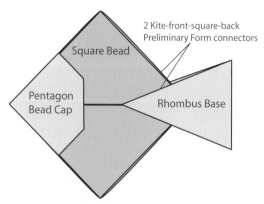

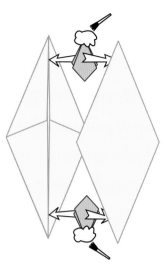

Here is a playful idea that uses a Square Bead, a Pentagon Bead Cap, two Kite-Front-Square-Back Preliminary Form Connectors, and a Rhombus Base (see opposite) to form a Fish-shaped bead or brooch.

Kite Front and Back Preliminary Form Connectors may be used to connect two Rhombus Bases, back to back.

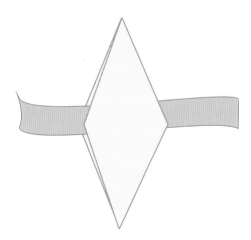

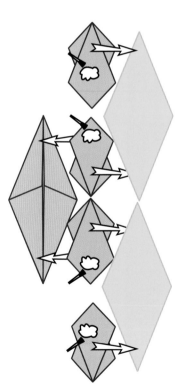

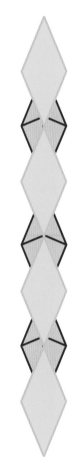

You may pass a ribbon through the open space for stringing.

Use the Opposed Kites Preliminary Form Connectors to build chains of alternating Rhombus Bases.

Here is a partial chain of alternating Rhombus Bases (see opposite). You may vary the size of the Rhombus Bases that make up the chain.

Rhombus Bases

This classic origami base will serve as a mounting and connecting fixture for our jewelry-making system. Use sturdy papers for strength. Do not place a crease running across the long diagonal of the final form; it would be distracting and it could weaken the piece.

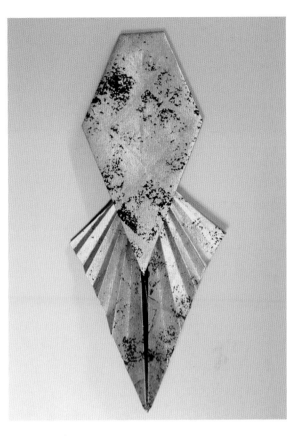

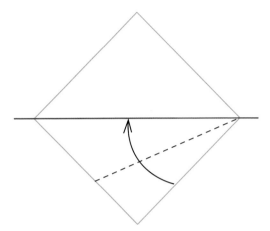

1. Begin with the non-display side up. Using a ruler or straightedge, determine the horizontal center diagonally. Mark this line with a pencil or simply hold the edge in place during the first fold. Valley-fold the bottom right edge up to this line.

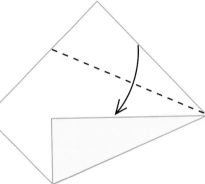

2. Valley-fold the top right edge to align with the edge at the center to form a kite shape.

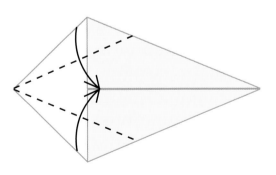

3. Valley-fold the top and bottom left edges to the centerline.

Slots for mounting

4. The completed Rhombus Base.

Triangle Beads

Designed by Michael G. LaFosse

This bead is simple to fold and quick to form, which is great if you are making dozens of beads, perhaps for a craft fair or bazaar. This simplicity allows the use of a wide range of papers. The Triangle Bead may be transformed into several new bead shapes that we call "morphs." We have named these morphs: Triangle, Barrel, Teardrop, Blossom, Flattened Barrel, and Lantern Beads.

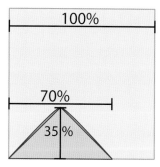

Two-inch (5-cm) squares will produce beads approximately 1½ inches (3.8 cm) long.

Make beads of any size by using different size squares. The wet-folded beads shape nicely when the paper is first back-coated with starch paste or methylcellulose paste applied between the two layers (see page 68).

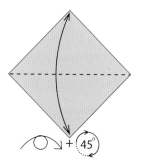

1. Begin with the display side facing up. Valley-fold in half, bottom corner to top. Unfold. Turn over and rotate 45 degrees.

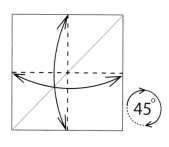

2. Valley-fold in half, edge to edge, both ways, unfolding after each. Rotate 45 degrees.

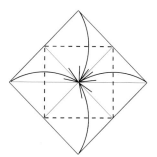

3. Valley-fold each corner to meet in the middle, where the creases intersect.

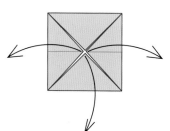

4. Unfold all but the top corner flap.

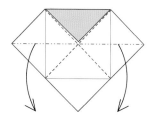

5. Use the existing mountain and valley creases to collapse the model, mountain-folding the left and right corners in half and moving them to the bottom corner.

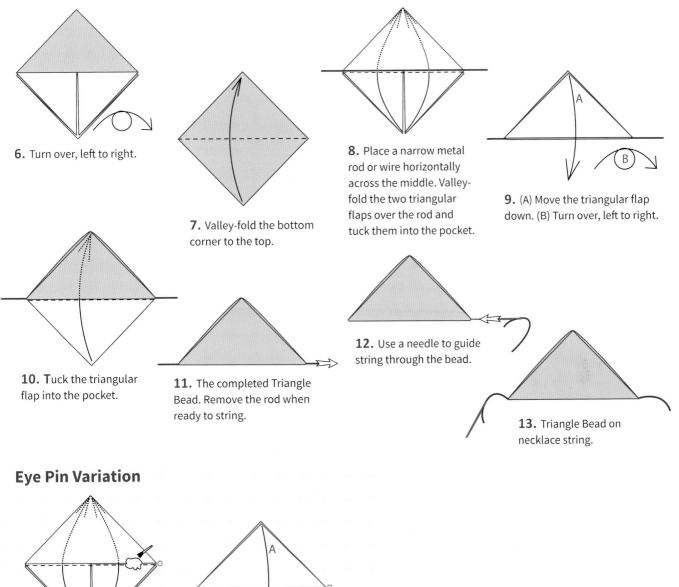

6. Turn over, left to right.

7. Valley-fold the bottom corner to the top.

8. Place a narrow metal rod or wire horizontally across the middle. Valley-fold the two triangular flaps over the rod and tuck them into the pocket.

9. (A) Move the triangular flap down. (B) Turn over, left to right.

10. Tuck the triangular flap into the pocket.

11. The completed Triangle Bead. Remove the rod when ready to string.

12. Use a needle to guide string through the bead.

13. Triangle Bead on necklace string.

Eye Pin Variation

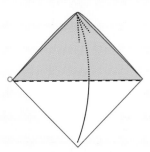

1. An eye pin may be pasted in place at step 8. If necessary, trim the length of the eye pin to fit the bead. Valley-fold the two triangular flaps over the eye pin and tuck them into the pocket.

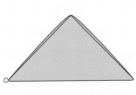

2. (A) Move the triangular flap down. (B) Turn over, left to right.

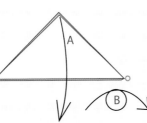

3. Tuck the triangular flap into the pocket.

4. The completed Triangle Bead with eye pin.

Triangle Beads drying on a wire.

Triangle Bead Morphs

Since the Triangle Bead's versatility allows you to morph it into many different forms, it is easy to add "related variety" when and where you need it.

Each of these forms results from opening the pocket(s) differently. See if you can discover even more of the many variations on your own! Most of these beads are best made with an eye pin installed as they are being folded (see Eye Pin Variation box on page 29) for use as drop-style beads. They may also be strung with a needle and beading wire or heavy thread. Use papers that have strong, flexible qualities, like many popular Asian papers, or even some plastic-coated papers. When you wet-fold these beads with paste, the shaping possibilities grow.

Barrel Beads

Designed by Michael G. LaFosse

Paper likes to be flat, but beads like to be round. The Barrel Bead morph was my first attempt at designing a rounded, cylindrical, yet sturdy bead that is substantial, attractive, and versatile. The rounded edges on each side of the barrel form perfect mounting sites for other beads of glass, stone, or plastic. Combine two or three Barrel Beads to form pendants. A 2-inch (5-cm) square will produce a bead that is 1½ inches (3.8 cm) long.

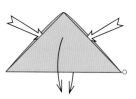

1. Begin with a Triangle Bead (page 28). Gently open each of the two pockets found along the short edges of the triangle. Press and spread open into a cylindrical shape. Smooth the two open oval edges all around, and form a neatly rounded symmetrical shape.

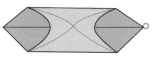

2. The completed Barrel Bead.

Flattened Barrel Beads

Designed by Michael G. LaFosse

Flattened Barrel Beads also display the paper's decorative features beautifully, and form versatile settings for other origami elements, since they contain pockets where tabs from the other elements may be inserted.

Flattened Barrel Beads are well-suited for use in bracelets because they lay flat against the skin without being bulky. When folded from stiff gold papers or foils, these flat barrel beads set off and protect more delicate origami jewelry elements. These also lend themselves to tiling with other square and triangular shapes.

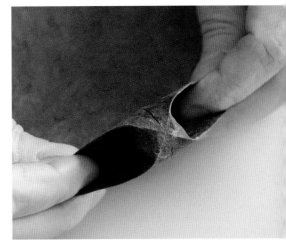

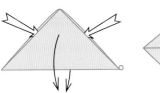 

1. Begin with a Triangle Bead (page 28). Gently open each of the two pockets found along the short edges of the triangle.

2. Press and spread the pockets open, first forming a cylindrical shape, and then, as you continue to flatten the center, it will form the shape of a square (with an "x" of creases collapsed in the center).

3. The completed Flattened Barrel Bead.

Lantern Beads

Designed by Michael G. LaFosse

This bead is three-dimensional, and crisply geometric. It acts as an angular antidote to the rounded Barrel Bead, so use it alternately when you wish to add a contrasting shape. These look especially "gemmy" when folded from foil-backed papers.

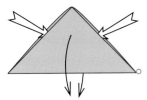 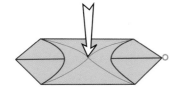 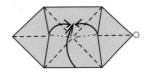 

1. Begin with a Triangle Bead (page 28). Gently open each of the two pockets found along the short edges of the triangle.

2. Press and spread open, first into the cylindrical shape, and then continue to flatten the center to form the shape of a square with an "x" in the middle.

3. Valley-fold the diagonals and mountain-fold the horizontals to form a hollow bow tie shape from the center square.

4. The completed Lantern Bead.

Teardrop Beads

Designed by Michael G. LaFosse

This bead reminds me of a faceted semiprecious stone, perhaps an agate or onyx. Its geometric style also provides contrast to the rounded Barrel Bead series, and it stands out nicely in an ensemble. The versatile shape works well in any orientation or combination, such as inverted, in joined pairs, chains, geometric groupings, or starbursts.

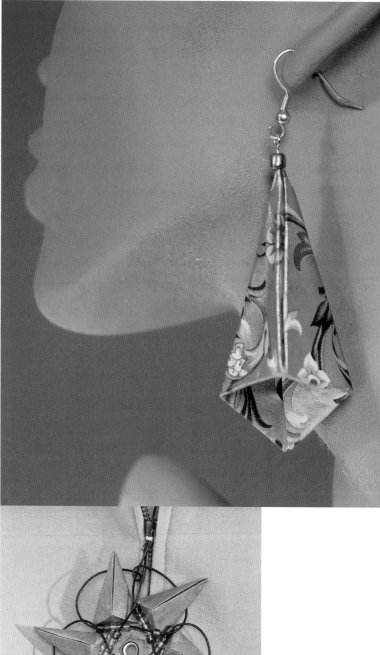

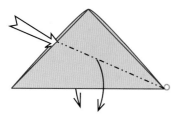

1. Begin with a Triangle Bead (page 28). Open only one of the two pockets on the short edges of the triangle. Spread and flatten the base into a triangular shape. Notice how a long pyramid forms on the top side. Sharpen the folded edges to form a neat, symmetrical, tapered prism.

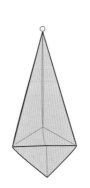

2. The completed Teardrop Bead.

Blossom Beads

Designed by Michael G. LaFosse

These beads represent couplets of flower petals, but when one sees an individual unit, it looked to me like a pair of mouse ears! You may catch me on the video calling it the Mouse Ear, a pet name used during design development, even though groups of them form beautiful, cascading masses of blossoms. In Hawai'i, floral leis typically contain hundreds of blossoms, and so we wanted a design that was simple and quick to fold. Inspiration for this design came during our exhibition in Waikiki, admiring favorite floral leis of numerous small white flowers. I did not want to copy the actual blossoms, which would have been too time-consuming and complex, but I did want to create a simple bead that would give the same effect when multiple units were combined and strung into cascading leis.

Don't restrict your use of this bead to lei making. Experiment with earrings and bracelets, necklaces and brooches. Each of the little pockets, or "ears," can serve as a vestibule for affixing a bead, glass crystal, or other interesting element. Mounted together, they form collars.

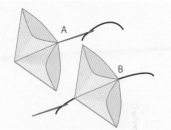

Stringing: (A) Using a needle and cord, pierce the center point from the open side of the Blossom Bead. (B) Push the needle through to the other side of the bead and pull the cord through.

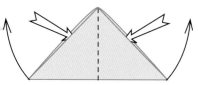

1. Begin with a Triangle Bead (page 28). Gently open each of the two pockets found along the short edges of the triangle to form hollow cones.

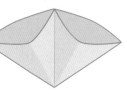

2. The completed Blossom Bead.

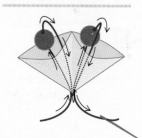

1. Stringing with round beads: Use needle and stringing cord to pierce from the outside bottom of one cup. Pass thread through the hole in the bead and run the thread out through the original thread hole in the bottom of the cup. Repeat with the other cup.

2. The Blossom Bead is held on to the stringing cord by the included beads.

Triangle Bead Morphs with Tabs

The flaps hidden inside all of the triangle beads (and morphs) can be pulled out, squashed, and put to use as versatile tab connectors. There are three tab set configurations, each with a strategic mounting purpose. These tabs fit into any bead unit containing slots. The diamond-shaped "tab sets" each consist of a squashed triangular flap. There will be a minimum of two triangular flaps and a maximum of four.

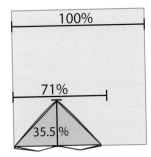

Triangle Bead Base with Two Square Tab Sets

All of the Triangle Bead morphs can be made from this base—with added mounting options. Use these tabs to connect different beads in a variety of combinations.

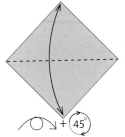

1. Begin with the display side up. Valley-fold in half, bottom corner to top. Unfold. Turn over and rotate 45 degrees.

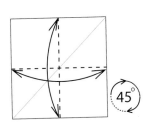

2. Valley-fold in half, edge to edge, both ways, unfolding after each. Rotate 45 degrees.

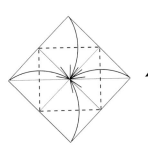

3. Valley-fold each corner to meet in the middle, where the creases intersect.

4. Unfold the left and right corner flaps.

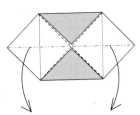

5. Use the existing mountain and valley creases to collapse the model, mountain-folding the left and right corners in half and moving them to the bottom corner.

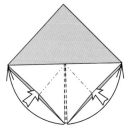

6. Inside-reverse-fold the two bottom flaps to form two sets of twin triangle flaps.

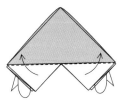

7. Valley-fold the triangular flaps to be perpendicular to the Triangle Bead.

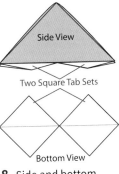

8. Side and bottom views: The completed Triangle Bead Base with Two Square Tab Sets.

Connecting Beads with Tabs

To use the Triangle Bead Base with Two Square Tab Sets to mount additional components, refer to the following sequence of photos.

1. Apply paste to each of the tab sets, or "feet."

2. Insert the pasted tabs, hiding them inside the slot as the two triangle beads are brought together.

3. Keep all of the components held tightly together until the paste sets.

Triangle Bead Base with One Square Tab Set

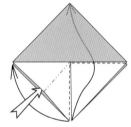
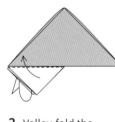
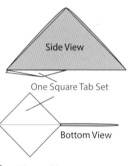

Side View

One Square Tab Set

Bottom View

1. Fold through step 5 on the facing page. Inside-reverse-fold only one triangular flap; valley-fold to tuck the other flap up inside the bead.

2. Valley-fold the triangular flaps to be perpendicular to the Triangle Bead.

3. Side and bottom views: The completed Triangle Bead Base with One Square Tab Set.

Triangle Bead Base with One Square Tab Set and One Triangular Tab

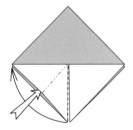
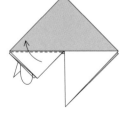
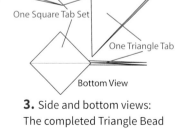

Side View

One Square Tab Set

One Triangle Tab

Bottom View

1. Fold through step 5 on the facing page. Inside-reverse-fold only one of the triangular flaps.

2. Valley-fold the triangular flaps to be perpendicular to the Triangle Bead.

3. Side and bottom views: The completed Triangle Bead Base with One Square Tab Set and One Triangular Tab.

To use the Triangle Bead Base with One Square Tab Set and One Triangular Tab to mount additional components, refer to the following sequence of photos, where tab sets on the pink bead perpendicularly suspend the red bead.

1. Apply paste to each of the two square-shaped tab sets, one on each lower half of the pink bead components.

2. With all components pasted, insert one tab set into the red bead, slide the other half of the pink bead close enough to insert the second tab set into the other side of the red bead.

3. The red bead pasted onto the pair of tab sets at the lower half of the pink bead.

Barrel Beads with Tabs

As with Triangle Beads, any morphs can also be connected with tabs.

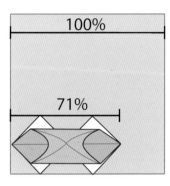

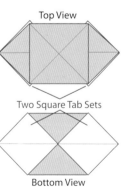

1. Fold through step 6 for the Triangle Bead Base with Two Square Tab Sets (page 34). Valley-fold the triangle flaps up on both sides.

2. Gently open each of the two pockets found along the short edges of the triangle. Press and spread open into a cylindrical shape. Smooth the edges all around, making a neatly rounded, symmetrical shape.

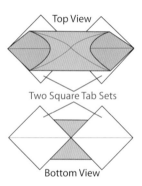

3. Top and bottom views: The completed Barrel Bead with Tabs (two square tab sets).

Flattened Barrel Beads with Tabs

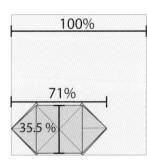

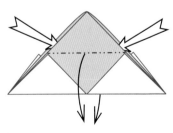

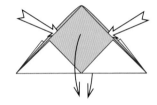

1. Fold step 1 for the Barrel Bead with Tabs (above). Gently open each of the two pockets found along the short edges of the triangle. Press and spread open into a cylindrical shape and then flatten.

2. Top and bottom views: The completed Flattened Barrel Bead with Tabs (two square tab sets).

Lantern Beads with Tabs

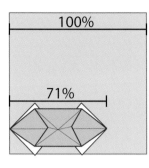

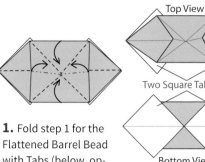

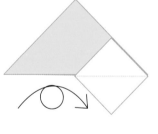

Top View

Two Square Tab Sets

Bottom View

1. Fold step 1 for the Flattened Barrel Bead with Tabs (below, opposite). Valley-fold the diagonals and mountain-fold the horizontals to form a hollow bow tie shape from the center square.

2. Top and bottom views: The completed Lantern Bead with Tabs (two square tab sets).

Teardrop Beads with Tabs

Let's learn the single tab set version of the Teardrop Bead first.

Teardrop Bead with One Square Tab Set

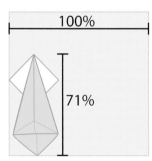

1. Fold through step 5 for the Triangle Bead with Tabs (page 34). Valley-fold the bottom left triangular flap up into the bead.

2. Squash-fold the remaining triangular flap up.

3. Your paper should look like this. Turn over, left to right.

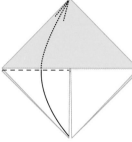

4. Gently open only the pocket at the end opposite the tab set. Press and spread open into an elongated pyramid.

90°

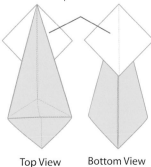

One Square Tab Set

5. Top and bottom views: The completed Teardrop Bead with Tabs (one square tab set at the top).

Top View   Bottom View

Teardrop Bead with Two Square Tab Sets

To use the Teardrop Bead with One Square Tab Set to mount additional components, refer to the following sequence of photos.

1. Apply paste to all tabs, including those for the Square Bead.

2. Insert the square tab of the Teardrop Bead at desired position.

3. Close the surrounding Square Bead elements and secure until dry.

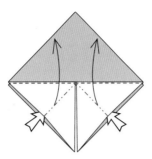

1. Fold through step 5 for the Triangle Bead with Tabs. Squash-fold each of the two triangular flaps up.

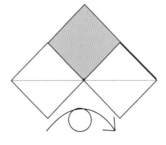

2. Your paper should look like this. Turn over, left to right.

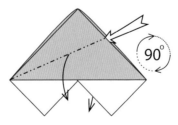

3. Gently open only one of the two pockets found along the short edges of the triangle. Press and spread open into an elongated pyramid.

Two Square Tab Sets

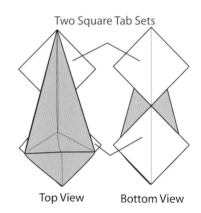

Top View   Bottom View

4. Top and bottom views: The completed Teardrop Bead with Two Square Tab Sets.

Preliminary Form Beads

Designed by Michael G. LaFosse

This bead unit can be best used when combined with other units. When a minimum of three identical units are combined, they produce a Collar Bead. Using five or more creates a corkscrew spiral shape.

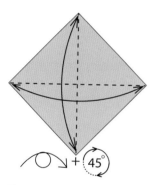

1. Begin with the display side up. Valley-fold in half diagonally both ways, unfolding after each. Turn over and rotate 45 degrees.

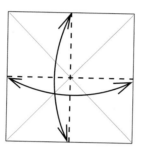

2. Valley-fold in half, edge to edge, both ways, unfolding after each.

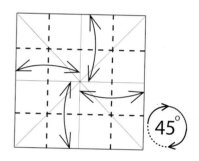

3. Valley-fold and unfold each of the four edges to the center. Rotate 45 degrees.

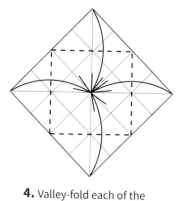

4. Valley-fold each of the four corners to the center.

5. Unfold only the left and right corners.

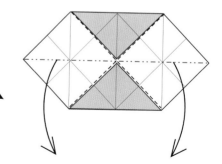

6. Use the existing mountain and valley creases to collapse the model, mountain-folding the left and right corners in half and moving them to the bottom corner.

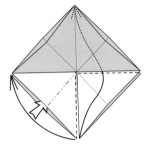

7. Inside-reverse-fold the bottom left triangle flap. Valley-fold the bottom right triangle flap up into the bead.

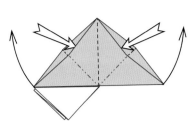

8. Open the top left and right pockets to form squared cones.

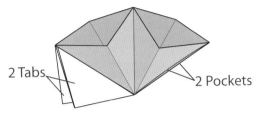

9. The completed Preliminary Form Bead with two tabs and two pockets. The pockets are slot-like.

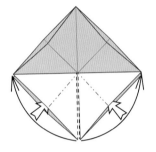

1. It is sometimes necessary to use a Preliminary Form Bead that has two sets of tabs. Fold through step 6 and then inside-reverse-fold both bottom tabs.

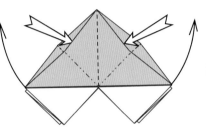

2. Open both pockets to form squared cones.

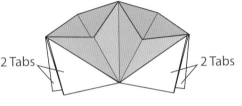

3. The completed Preliminary Form Bead with two sets of tabs.

Collar Bead

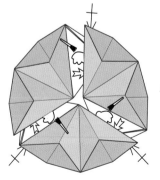

1. Joining three Preliminary Form Beads builds a Collar Bead. Apply glue to the tabs. Insert the tabs of one bead into the pockets of another. Four joined beads are possible as well.

2. The complete Collar Bead. String through the hole in the center.

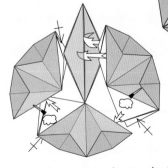

1. A Collar Bead can be attached to a Square Bead. Notice that you will need one Preliminary Form Bead that has two sets of tabs (purple diagram) to complete the circuit.

2. The completed Collar Bead attached to a Square Bead.

Arrowhead Beads

Designed by Michael G. LaFosse

The Arrowhead Bead is similar in design to the Trident Bead, and is formed by squashing opposite points of the same base. It has an Art Deco style that contrasts well with other square beads, and complements other geometric jewelry and outfits. The stylized design harkens back to our primitive past when similar shapes were expertly carved from flint and worn on the body; kept handy while being useful adornments.

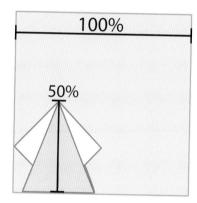

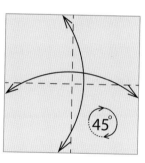

1. If using a two-colored sheet, begin with the major color side up. Valley-fold in half, edge to edge, both ways, unfolding after each. Rotate 45 degrees.

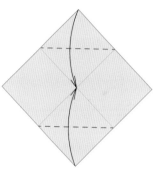

2. Valley-fold the top and bottom corners to meet at the center where the creases cross.

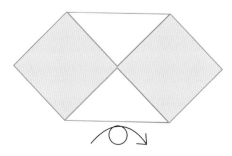

3. Turn over, left to right.

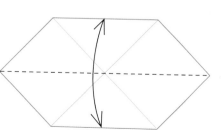

4. Valley-fold in half, bottom edge to top. Unfold, returning the edge to the bottom.

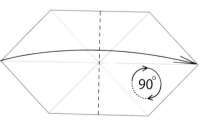

5. Valley-fold in half, corner to corner. Rotate 90 degrees clockwise.

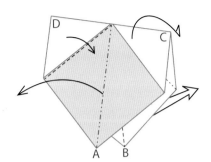

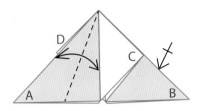

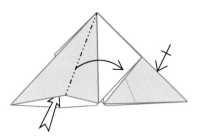

6. Mountain-fold corners A and B in half. Valley-fold corner D to lay upon A, and corner C to lay upon B. Look ahead at the next step for the shape.

7. Valley-fold the long edge of flap A to align with the vertical center. Unfold. Repeat behind with flap B.

8. Open the left flap and squash-fold to center. Repeat behind. Look ahead at the next step for the shape.

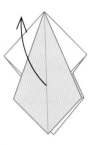

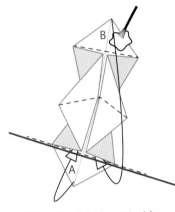

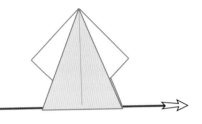

9. Lift up to open.

10. Valley-fold flap A inside the model. Apply paste to the inside of flap B, close the bead and insert flap B into the same pocket as flap A. You may also insert a wire before gluing in place, to create and open channel for stringing after the glue or paste dries.

11. Remove the wire when ready for stringing.

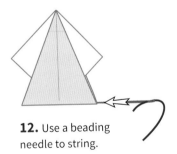

12. Use a beading needle to string.

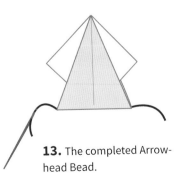

13. The completed Arrowhead Bead.

Owl Beads

An Arrowhead Bead variation by Deb Pun

Deb Pun—a long-time resident of the Big Island, a dear friend, and a tireless volunteer for OrigamiUSA—folded jewelry with us as we were developing some of these designs while tending our "Origami Do Experience" attraction in Hawaiʻi. Instead of folding the triangular flaps inside the Arrowhead Bead, she pasted them to the outside, forming a stylized owl shape.

Last spring a family of screech owlets frequented our place in Massachusetts and perched along the upper deck to supervise the nocturnal mammalian activity in the front lawn along the riverbank. Investigating a strange noise one night, I shined a flashlight into the darkness, only to be greeted by five pairs of glowing red eyes, all lined up along the rail! This experience inspired Richard Alexander to install red seed beads for eyes, and gold pins for pupils.

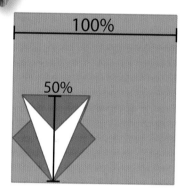

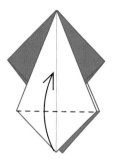

1. Begin with an Arrowhead Bead folded to step 9. Valley-fold the bottom square corner of the top layer up to form a triangular flap.

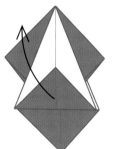

2. Lift up to open.

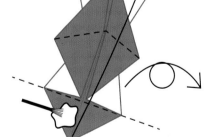

3. Apply paste to the inside of the bottom triangular flap, close the bead, and insert the pasted flap into the pocket. As with the Arrowhead Bead, you may also insert a wire at this time to preserve a path for a future needle and beading string.

4. The completed Owl Bead. For a more literal representation, affix red seed beads to the upper flap with escutcheon pins.

Twin Arrowhead Beads

Designed by Michael G. LaFosse

Simply combining two Arrowhead Beads forms a lantern-shaped cage, ideal for pendants or drop earrings. The void provides a niche for a precious bead or miniature origami object. (Be sure to use sturdy papers!)

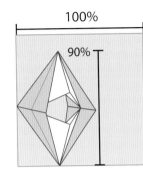

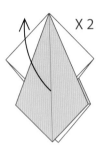

1. Begin with two Arrowhead Beads folded to step 9 (page 41). Lift up to open both.

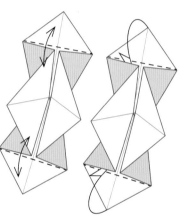

2. Valley-fold and unfold the top and bottom triangular flaps of one unit. Valley-fold the top and bottom triangular flaps of the other unit inside the model.

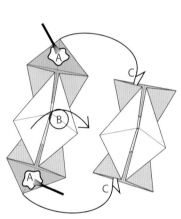

3. (A) Apply paste to the areas indicated in blue on one of the units. (B) Turn the pasted unit to face the open side of the other unit. (C) Insert the pasted triangular flaps into the open pockets.

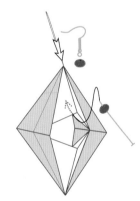

4. The completed Twin Arrowhead Bead. To add mounting wire for an earring, you will need for each: 1 Head Pin, 2 small round beads, earring finding, a wire cutter and round nose pliers. Use the needle to pierce a small hole in the top of the Twin Arrowhead Bead. Add one round bead to the bottom of the head pin. Pass the headpin through the hole in the Twin Arrowhead Bead from the inside.

5. Add the other round bead to the head pin and cut the protruding wire to length in preparation for forming an eye.

6. Use round nose pliers to form an eye at the protruding end of the wire. Attach earring finding to the eye.

7. The Mounted Twin Arrowhead Bead earring.

Duo Kite Beads

Designed by Michael G. LaFosse

This striking duo-colored geometric composition produced by folding a single square epitomizes the magic of origami. So simple. So clean. So attractive!

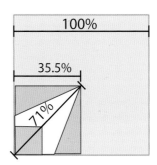

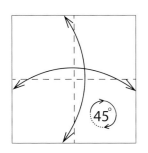

1. If using a two-colored sheet, begin with the major color side up. Valley-fold in half, edge to edge, both ways, unfolding after each. Rotate 45 degrees.

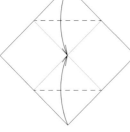

2. Valley-fold the top and bottom corners to meet at the center where the creases cross.

3. Turn over, left to right.

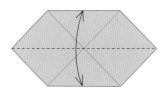

4. Valley-fold in half, bottom edge to top. Unfold, returning the edge to the bottom.

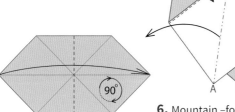

5. Valley-fold in half, corner to corner. Rotate 90 degrees clockwise.

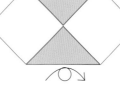

6. Mountain –fold corners A and B in half. Valley-fold corner D to lay upon A, and corner C to lay upon B. Look ahead at the next step for the shape.

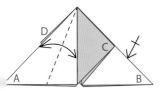

7. Valley-fold the long edge of flap A to align with the vertical center. Unfold. Repeat behind with flap B.

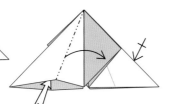

8. Open the left flap and squash-fold to center. Repeat behind. Look ahead at the next step for the shape.

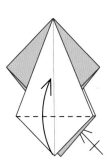

9. Valley-fold the bottom square corner of the top layer up. Repeat behind.

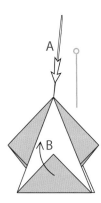

10. (A) Using a needle, pierce the top corner to make a small hole for the insertion of an eye pin. (B) Open the paper from the bottom.

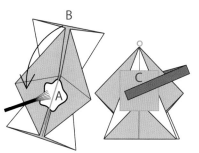

11. (A) Apply paste and insert the eye pin through the hole in the top of the model. (B) Close the model. (C) Keep the paper closed and flat with a small clamp, paperclip, or a clothespin. To prevent the clamp from making dents in the model, place small squares of thin card between the jaws of the clamp and the paper. Allow the glue to dry.

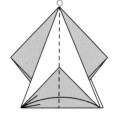

12. When dry, valley-fold the tall triangular form on the front in half, right to left.

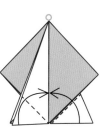

13. Valley-fold the bottom left and right corners up.

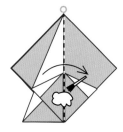

14. Apply paste and valley-fold the topmost left layer to the right. Look ahead for the shape.

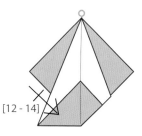

[12 - 14]

15. Repeat steps 12 through 14 on the left.

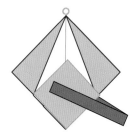

16. Clamp or apply a gentle weight and let the glue dry.

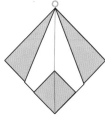

17. The completed Duo Kite Bead.

Trident Beads

Designed by Michael G. LaFosse

This flat bead has a more complex look than most of the other beads in this book, even though it is just as quick to fold. It is a good bead to use in concert with related designs, such as the Arrowhead Bead. Use paper that is colored differently on each side for the two-color variation explained at the end of the Trident Bead video instruction on the DVD. Notice how different looks are possible with subtle shaping.

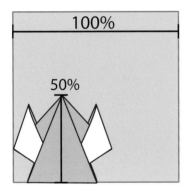

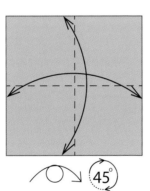

1. Begin with the major color side facing up. Valley-fold in half, edge to edge both ways, unfolding after each. Turn over and rotate 45 degrees.

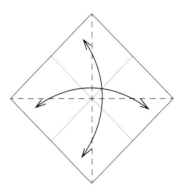

2. Valley-fold in half diagonally, corner to corner both ways, unfolding after each.

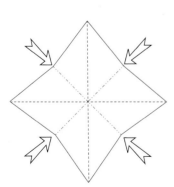

3. Use the mountain and valley creases to collapse the form into a four-point star. Flatten the model into a triangle with two flaps on the left and the right.

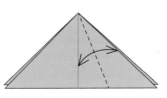

4. Pre-crease by valley-folding the long edge of the top right flap to the middle of the paper. Unfold.

5. Open the flap and flatten it into a kite-shape, centered on the model.

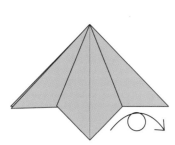

6. Turn over, left to right.

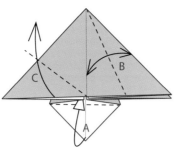

7. (A) Valley-fold the bottom square corner into the model. (B) Valley-fold the long edge of the top right flap to the middle. Unfold. (C) Valley-fold the left flap up at an outward angle. Look ahead at the next step to see the resulting shape.

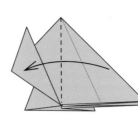

8. Move the top right flap to the left.

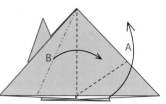

9. (A) Valley-fold the right flap up at an outward angle to match the similar flap of the left. (B) Open the top left flap and flatten into a kite-shape.

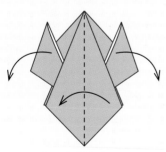

10. Turn over, left to right.

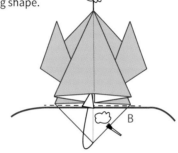

11. (A) You may install an eye pin through the top corner. Or (B) Trap beading string, or a wire rod placeholder for later stringing, at the flap end of the model. In either case, apply paste to the bottom flap and tuck it into the bottom pocket, locking the bead.

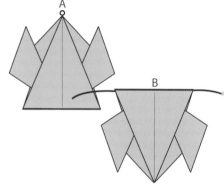

12. (A) The completed Trident Bead with eye pin. (B) The completed Trident Bead on string.

Color Change Variation

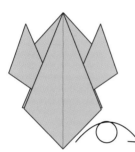

1. Fold a Trident Bead up to step 10, without turning the model over. Move the left and right side pointed flaps down. Valley-fold the right half of the kite-shape to the left.

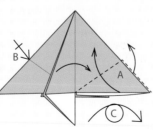

2. (A) Outside-reverse fold the right side flap, using the creases as a guide. Return the kite flap to the right. (B) Repeat on the left. (C) Turn over, left to right.

3. Paste and tuck the bottom corner flap into the model to lock it.

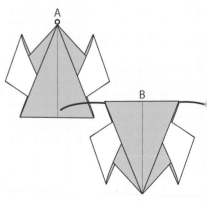

4. The completed Trident Bead with color change. (A) and (B) show different mounting options.

Wolverine Claws

Designed by Richard L. Alexander

This unusual design is a modern echo of our earliest of jewelry—a keepsake tooth or claw of the beast, vanquished after ravaging the village or camp ... the hunting souvenir ceremonially presented to the brave victor who wore it with pride. It is simple, abstract, and bold, transforming even the most humble patterned paper into a conversation piece! The finishing steps take the model from flat to fat in a most satisfying way. The structure is designed to be reinforced not only by the pleasing, final shape, but by the internal pleats and angles. As a singular pendant, or as a group of graduated sizes arranged in starbursts, these lightweight components can be folded in any size you desire. Larger models from bold prints work well as hair clasp decorations, or on chopsticks or hatpins worn as a fashion statement. Since the finished model is hollow, be sure to use stiff, well-sized and back-coated papers.

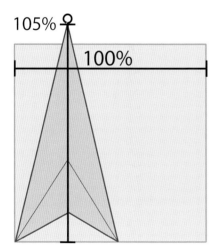

105% 100%

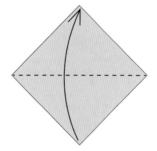

1. Begin display side up. Valley-fold in half, bottom corner to top.

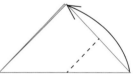

2. Valley-fold the bottom right corner to the top corner, forming a triangular flap.

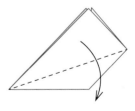

4. Valley-fold the top flap down, as far as it will go, flat.

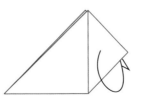

3. Reverse the triangular flap to the back.

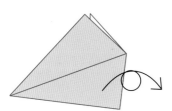

5. Turn over, left to right.

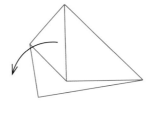

6. Unfold the triangular flap on the left.

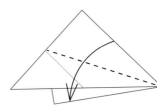

7. Valley-fold the top flap down to match the position of the flap at the back.

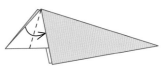

8. Valley-fold the indicated double edge to align with the short edge of the top layer triangle flap.

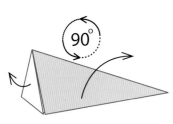

9. Unfold completely and rotate 90 degrees counter clockwise.

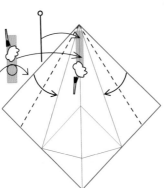

10. Check the crease pattern, your paper should look like this. This is the best time to add mounting hardware, such as an eye pin. Apply paste to a narrow strip of paper and paste it over the pin. Valley-fold the two top edges, each to the nearest crease. Allow the paste to dry.

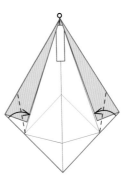

11. Valley-fold the indicated edges to the target creases in the previous step.

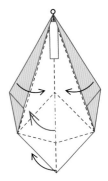

12. Inside View: Use the existing creases to close the bead.

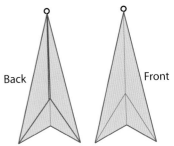

Back   Front

13. The completed Wolverine Claw, front and back.

Abstract Sail Elements

This versatile, trapezoidal box element has lines that conjure a stiff breeze along the windward side near Kaneohe Bay. Its dynamic angles will make you look like you are indeed "going places." The several congruent pockets allow nesting smaller versions for added interest, and you are sure to have fun exploring how these versatile forms can be combined in countless ways.

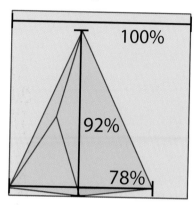

100%

92%

78%

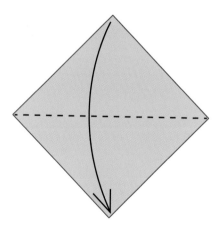

1. Begin with the display side up. Valley-fold in half, top corner to bottom.

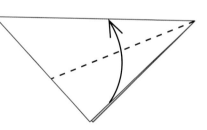

2. Valley-fold the bottom right edge of the top layer to the long top edge.

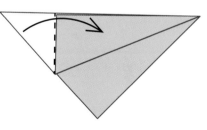

3. Valley-fold the left side triangular flap over the top layer.

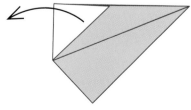

4. Unfold the last step.

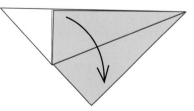

5. Unfold the top layer flap.

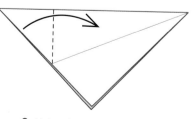

6. Using the existing crease, valley fold the left side triangular flap to the right.

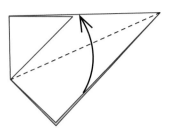

7. Valley-fold the bottom triangle flap up to lock the layers.

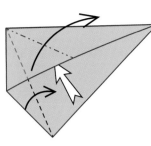

8. Open the pocket and move the top layers, swiveling up and to the right, and then flatten.

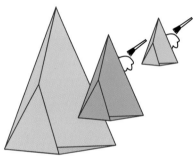

9. Open the pocket and square the creases to form an open space.

10. The completed Abstract Sail Element. It may be oriented in any direction for final display.

Abstract Sail Element Brooch

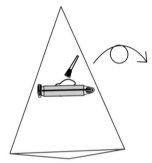

1. Make a simple brooch by gluing a pin back to the back of the Abstract Sail Element. Turn over, to display the front.

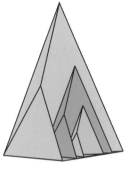

2. Additional smaller Sail Elements may be glued inside the brooch.

3. The completed multi-unit Abstract Sail Element Brooch.

Two-Element Brooch

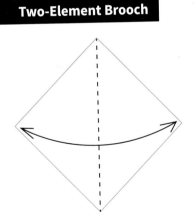

1. Two same-sized Abstract Sail Elements may be joined using a simple origami connector. Use a square that is the same size as the paper used to fold the Abstract Sail Elements. Valley-fold in half diagonally and unfold.

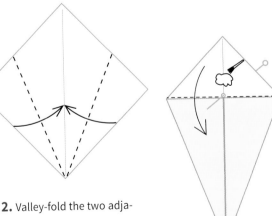

2. Valley-fold the two adjacent bottom edges to meet at the vertical crease.

3. If adding an eye pin, pierce the paper as indicated and glue the pin in place. Valley-fold the top triangle flap down.

4. Your connector should look like this. Turn over, left to right.

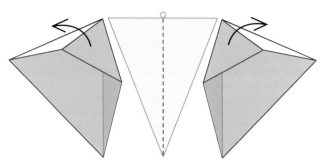
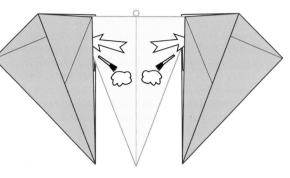

1. Connect two Abstract Sail Elements by first flattening them so that the long, overlapped flap edges are easy to access. Install a vertical valley crease up the middle of the connector.

2. Insert one half of the connector behind the long triangle flap of an Abstract Sail Element. Repeat with the other half of the connector on the other element. Use paste to ensure a permanent attachment.

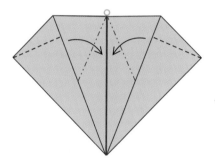

3. Open the Abstract Sail Elements to their 3-D form.

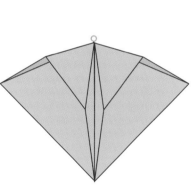

4. The completed pendant, using two Abstract Sail Elements and one connector.

Abstract Sail Element Earrings

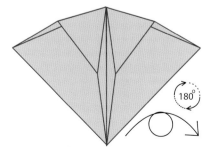

1. Make earrings by first connecting two Abstract Sail Elements as described above, but without the eye pin. Turn over and rotate so that the narrow corner is topmost.

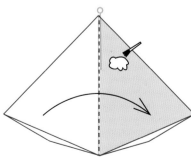

2. Apply paste to one side and install an eye pin into the top corner. Valley-fold in half.

3. Attach earring hardware to complete the Abstract Sail Element Earrings.

Angel Wings

Simple pleats formed by fan-folding or spin-folding generate interesting proportions and angles—not only in the paper, but in the elegant shadows they cast. See how elegant a combination of Angel Wings and a Rhombus Base, folded from fine papers that have first been back-coated, can look! The added layers strengthen the piece, while the simple design nicely displays the fancy paper patterns.

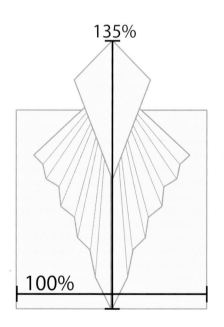

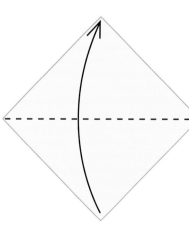

1. Begin with the display side facing up. Valley-fold in half, bottom corner to top.

2. Valley-fold the bottom right corner to the top corner.

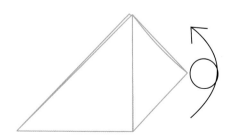

3. Turn over, bottom to top.

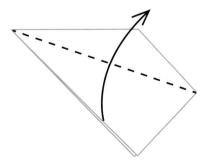

4. Valley-fold the top layer up, as far as it will go, flat.

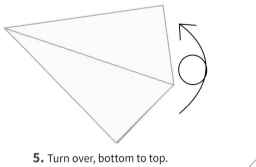

5. Turn over, bottom to top.

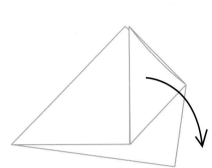

6. Fold the top triangle flap down.

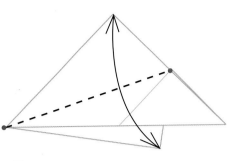

7. Valley-fold the top corner down to meet the bottommost corner. Your fold should span the distance between the crease ends, marked with red dots. Return the flap to the top.

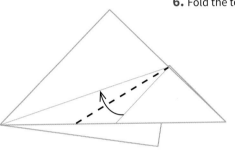

8. You will see two creases. Valley-fold the right corner up, laying the lower crease upon the upper crease.

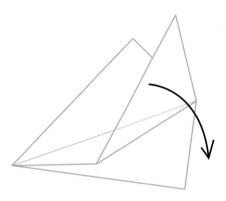

9. Your paper should look like this. Return the flap to the bottom.

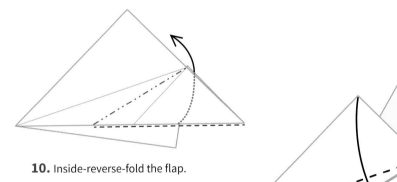

10. Inside-reverse-fold the flap.

11. Use the existing crease to valley-fold the indicated corner down to meet with the lowest corner.

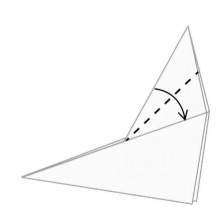

12. Valley-fold the long folded edge of the small triangle flap to align with the long folded edge of the large triangle flap.

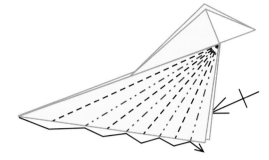

13. Unfold the last step.

14. Inside-reverse-fold the small triangle flap.

15. Fan-fold the large triangular flap. You may make any number of pleats that suit your design. Repeat with the large triangular flap on the other side.

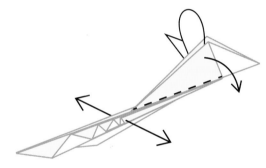

16. Unfold the fans. Spread open the inside reverse fold to form a kite.

17. The completed Angel Wings, front view.

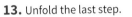

Rhombus-Base-Mounted Angel Wings

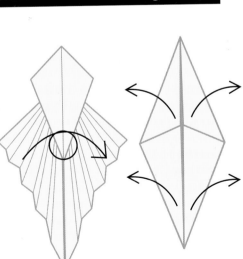

1. Make a mount by folding a Rhombus Base (see page 27) from the same size square that you used to fold the Angel Wings. Unfold the Rhombus Base and turn the Angel Wings display side toward the inside of the open Rhombus Base.

2. Apply paste to the inside of the open Rhombus Base. Align the kite section of the Angel Wings into the bottom corner of the Rhombus.

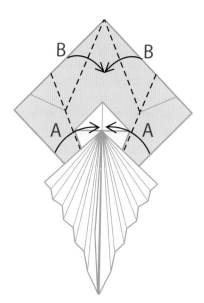

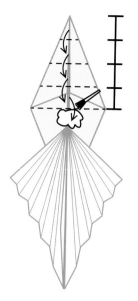

3. (A) Use the existing creases to valley-fold the bottom left and right edges of the open Rhombus Base around the kite, trapping it inside. (B) Use the existing creases to valley-fold the top of the Rhombus Base closed.

4. Apply paste just below the horizontal center of the Rhombus Base. Valley-fold the top half of the Rhombus Base down, over and over, dividing it in fourths and finally contacting the paste. This folded section forms a mounting loop.

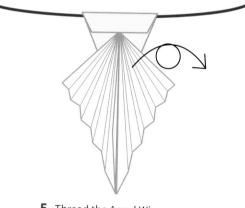

5. Thread the Angel Wings construction onto your beading wire or chain. Turn over.

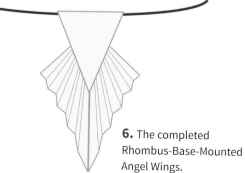

6. The completed Rhombus-Base-Mounted Angel Wings.

Slinking Triangle Beads

Designed by Richard L. Alexander

While pre-creasing several strips of decorative paper, I found myself fiddling with a long, trapezoidal remnant strip of beautiful handmade paper. I used a similar folding method to create a series of smaller and smaller triangles, threading and separating each layer with beads. The result was a curved, slinking drop that grew when I loosened the thread, or curled when I tightened it. There was a happy mid-point where it bounced a bit, but not to the point of deciding what it wanted to do!

2. Identify the 90-degree corner of the 1⅛-inch (2.9 cm) edge and move it to match the adjacent long edge, forming a triangular flap.

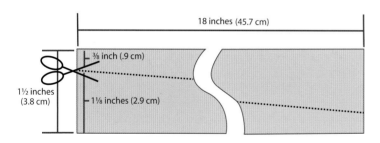

1. Cut a strip of back-coated, decorative duo (two-colored) paper 1½ inches (3.8 cm) wide by 18 inches long. Cut the strip in half lengthwise, beginning at ⅜ inch (.9 cm) at one end and widening to 1⅛ inches (2.9 cm) at the other, making two identically tapered trapezoidal strips.

3. Mountain-fold the triangular area behind the strip. You will end up with a straight folded-edge with a 90-degree corner at one end.

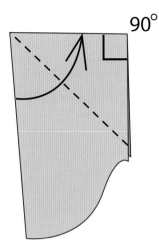

90°

4. Valley-fold the opposite long edge to the top edge.

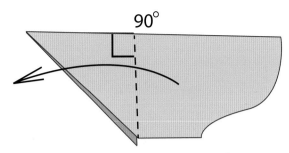
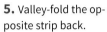

90°

5. Valley-fold the opposite strip back.

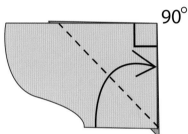

90°

6. Valley-fold the strip up. Continue in this manner until the strip is used up.

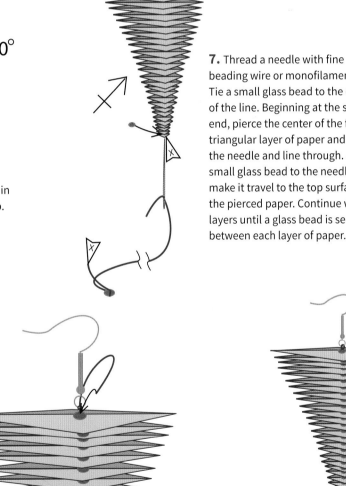

7. Thread a needle with fine beading wire or monofilament. Tie a small glass bead to the end of the line. Beginning at the small end, pierce the center of the first, triangular layer of paper and pass the needle and line through. Add a small glass bead to the needle and make it travel to the top surface of the pierced paper. Continue with all layers until a glass bead is secured between each layer of paper.

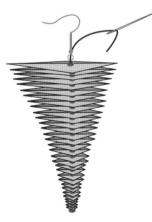

8. Thread one last bead for the top, and then pass the needle and line through the eye of a jewelry mount, such as an earring or a jump ring.

9. Securely tie the line to the jewelry mount and pass the remnant of the line down through the holes and beads in the top of the piece to hide it.

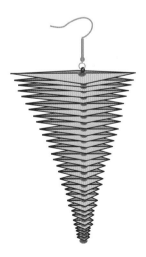

10. The completed Slinking Triangle Bead.

Square Jewelry Gift Box and Lid

Traditional design

After you make your origami jewelry, you will want to present it in an attractive package. Why not use the same fancy paper to fold a beautiful, color-coordinated gift box? This square box is also called the *masu* in Japanese, because it is reminiscent of the wooden box by that same name used for measuring. A masu is also used to serve sake, a fermented rice wine, during celebrations.

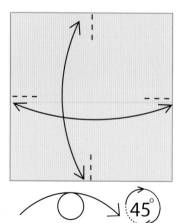

1. Begin with the colored side up. Mark the center of each of the four edges of the square with short valley creases. Turn over and rotate 45 degrees.

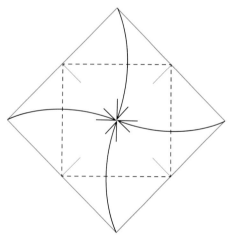

2. Blintz-fold by valley-folding each of the four corners to meet at the middle. You will use the short creases to guide you.

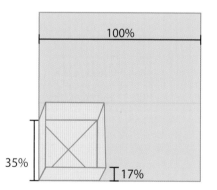

3. Valley-fold the top and bottom edges to meet at the middle. Unfold.

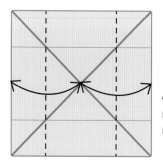

4. Valley-fold the left and right edges to meet at the middle. Unfold.

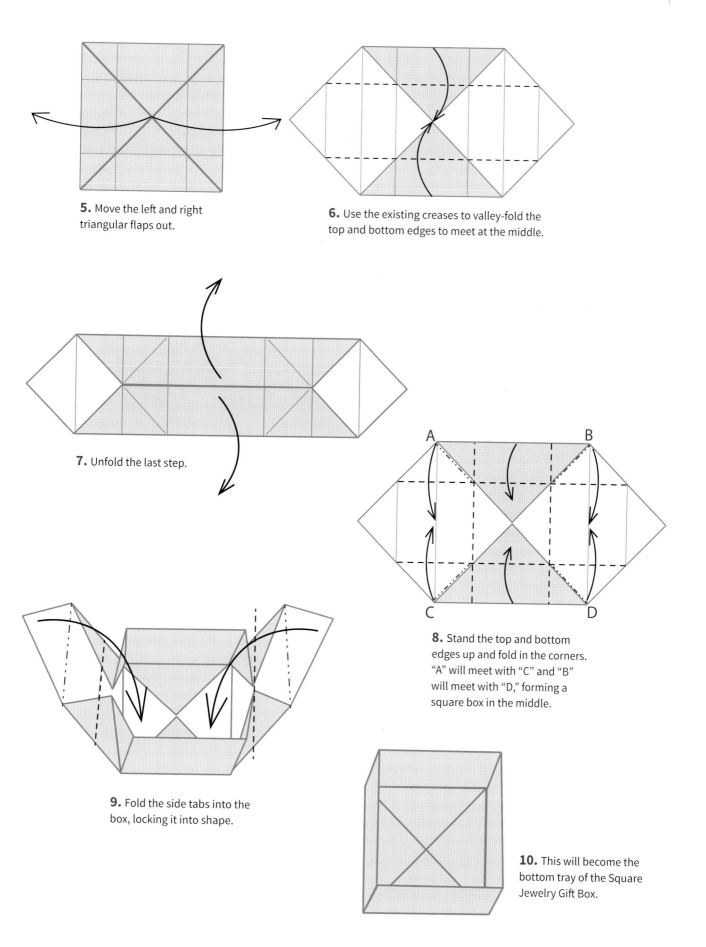

5. Move the left and right triangular flaps out.

6. Use the existing creases to valley-fold the top and bottom edges to meet at the middle.

7. Unfold the last step.

8. Stand the top and bottom edges up and fold in the corners. "A" will meet with "C" and "B" will meet with "D," forming a square box in the middle.

9. Fold the side tabs into the box, locking it into shape.

10. This will become the bottom tray of the Square Jewelry Gift Box.

Square Jewelry Gift Box Lid

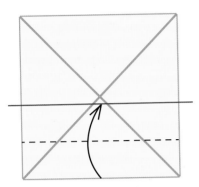

1. To make a lid for this box, use another square of the same size as the one used for the bottom. Fold through step 3. Valley-fold the bottom edge up to fall about ¼ inch (.7 cm) below the center.

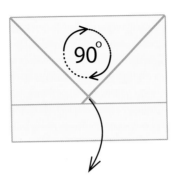

2. Unfold this rectangular flap and let it take the attached triangle flap with it. Rotate the paper 45 degrees clockwise.

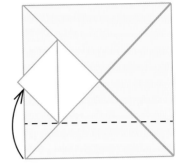

3. Valley-fold the new bottom edge up to the level where the lower edge of the triangular flap intersects the vertical left edge of the square.

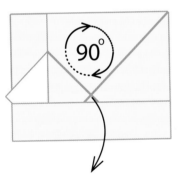

4. Unfold this new rectangular flap and let it take the attached triangular flap with it. Rotate the paper 45 degrees clockwise.

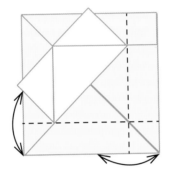

5. Valley-fold and unfold the remaining two edges in the same manner.

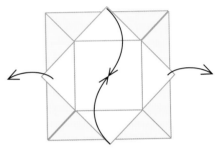

6. Your paper should look like this. Pull the left and right corners out. Move the top and bottom corners to meet at the center.

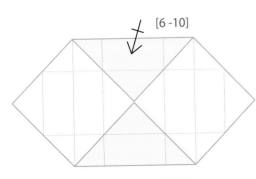

[6 -10]

7. Repeat steps 6 through 10 from page 61 to make the box lid three-dimensional.

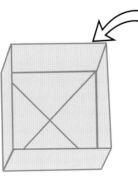

8. Place the lid on the bottom tray.

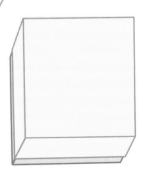

9. The completed Square Jewelry Gift Box with Lid.

Long Jewelry Gift Box and Lid

Traditional design

Long rectangular origami boxes are much less common than square boxes, probably because they are seldom folded from a square, and therefore require measurement and calculation. We offered a chapter on designing rectangular origami boxes in our *Japanese Paper Crafting* book (Tuttle Publishing), and there we show how to quickly design any rectangular origami box. The lid is simply a slightly larger box, albeit shallower.

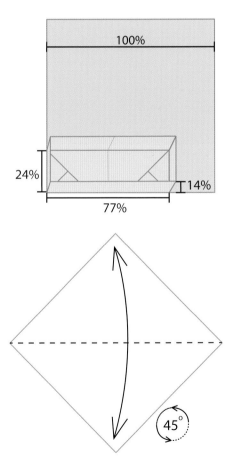

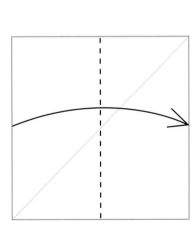

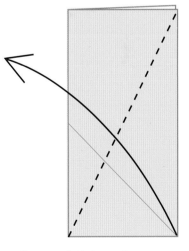

1. Begin with the non-display side facing up. Valley-fold in half diagonally, bottom corner to top. Unfold. Rotate 45 degrees counterclockwise.

2. The diagonal crease should span the bottom left and top right corners. Valley-fold in half, left edge to right edge.

3. Valley-fold the top layer diagonally by moving the bottom right corner up and to the left, guiding the crease to span the bottom left and top right corners.

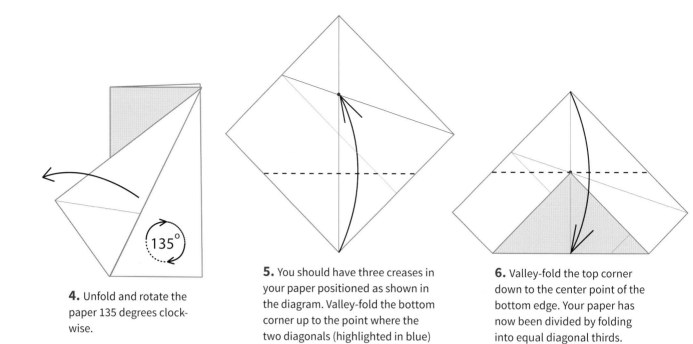

4. Unfold and rotate the paper 135 degrees clockwise.

5. You should have three creases in your paper positioned as shown in the diagram. Valley-fold the bottom corner up to the point where the two diagonals (highlighted in blue) intersect.

6. Valley-fold the top corner down to the center point of the bottom edge. Your paper has now been divided by folding into equal diagonal thirds.

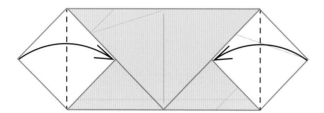

7. Valley-fold the left and right corners in to meet a point where two edges intersect.

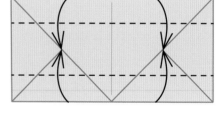

8. Your paper is now a 1:2 rectangle. Valley-fold the top and bottom long edges to meet at the horizontal center.

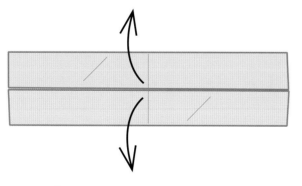

9. Unfold the last step.

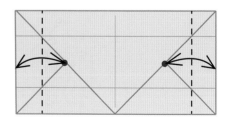

10. Valley-fold the left and right short edges in to the point where two edges intersect, indicated by the red dots. Return the short edges to the outside.

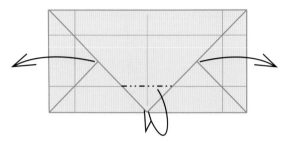

11. Unfold the left and right corners. Mountain-fold the indicated square corner level with the bottom horizontal crease line.

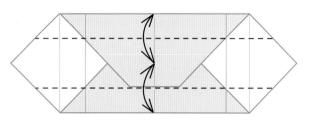

12. Sharpen the full length of the existing top and bottom horizontal creases by valley-folding and unfolding.

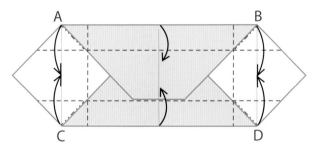

13. Stand the top and bottom edges up and fold in the corners. "A" will meet with "C" and "B" will meet with "D," forming a rectangular box in the middle.

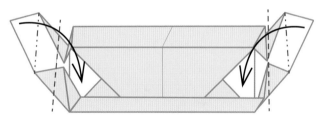

14. Use the existing creases to valley and mountain-fold the short sidewalls over the top edge and down to the inside floor.

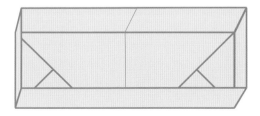

15. The completed box. This will serve as the bottom tray of the gift box.

Long Jewelry Gift Box Lid

[1 - 7]

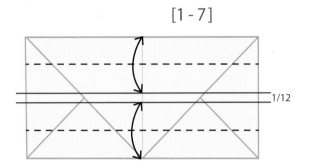

16. To make a lid for this box with no extraneous creases, fold a scrap square of paper (the same size as the one used for the bottom) through step 6. Lay the fancy top paper (also the same size as the one used for the bottom) on a template square, and match the shape. Fold step 7 from page 64, then valley-fold the top and bottom edges to leave a centered gap that measures 1/12 of the short edge of the folded rectangle. You may estimate this, but it is easy to measure and calculate.

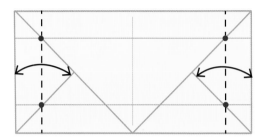

17. The left and right edges must be folded in to become the same height as the long walls. It is easy to find this measure: make your left and right valley folds intersect the places where the long horizontal creases from step 16 intersect the 45-degree-angled edges of paper, indicated here with red dots. Return the short edges to the outside.

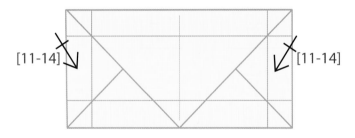

18. Repeat steps 11 through 14 from page 65.

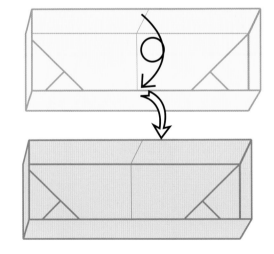

19. Fit the lid onto the box.

20. The completed Long Jewelry Gift Box with Lid.

Papers and Materials

When selecting papers for the projects in this book, consider how you intend to use the piece, and where and when you will use it.

Above: Colorful handmade papers, such as these rolls from the Origamido Studio, are made with high quality fibers and pigments.
Below: Fancy store-bought prints and patterns can be back-coated to make them suitable for folded "jewels."

If you are folding for family fun, paper selection might not be important, but if you are making pieces to wear for formal events, special gifts, or for sale, start with purchasing good quality, hand-made washi-style mulberry or abaca papers. They come in many weights, but stocking three different thicknesses—tissue thin, medium, and heavyweight—will generally cover your origami jewelry needs. Watercolor papers of 100 percent cotton rag are also useful, particularly if you choose the lightest weights. Be prepared to "buy and try" several types from convenient sources, and so don't buy much of any stock until you have had a chance to fold, test, and become familiar with a small sample.

Why limit yourself to folding just paper? Other foldable materials now exist that are more durable than the average paper off the shelf. Consider using vinyl wallpaper, plasticized or metallized films, foils, back-coated fabrics, or specialty composites. Laminates of these with fine handmade papers may be more decorative and durable than the paper alone, and yet still hold a crease well enough to allow using the origami techniques presented here. There are also thousands of dollar bill money folds, and many of these wonderfully tough paper currency compositions could easily become wearable art or jewelry.

Back-Coating the Paper

Back-coating is a popular technique for bonding sheets of paper to change their look, durability, or folding property. You may have a piece of beautiful paper that is too thin or weak, and by applying another layer of strong paper, you can use the display paper without worry. Perhaps you have two different colors that would look great together when folded into a project that reveals both colors. Back-coating allows you to combine them into a single sheet with a different color on each side. Most importantly, back-coating allows you to create a tough laminate with a layer of water-reversible paste between the papers, which becomes pliable when moistened. When dried, the folded paper retains its shape because the paste has stiffened.

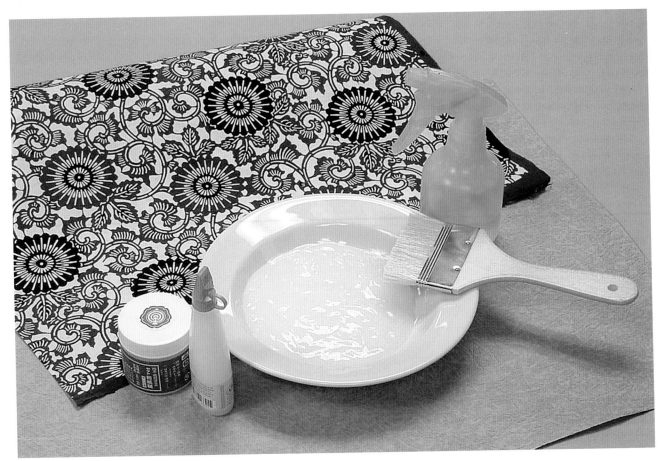

Materials List
- Two sheets of paper (a front piece and a backing sheet)
- Starch-based paste
- Small scrap of paper

Equipment
- Paste brush (China Bristle; 3 in / 7 cm) to apply the paste
- Paste bowl
- Spray bottle filled with water
- Drying board (Foamcore, plywood, glass, or other stiff material larger than the largest of your chosen papers)

1. Trim one of the two sheets to be approximately ½ inch (1.25 cm) shorter than the backing sheet on all sides. If the two sheets differ in thickness, trim the thicker sheet to be smaller. Lightly mist the papers on both sides. Allow a few moments for the moisture to be absorbed into the paper, causing it to expand. Adding water to the paper first prevents puckering when paste is applied. Since paste contains water, dry paper would pull water out of the paste, thickening the paste and making it difficult to spread.

2. Lay the larger sheet against the surface of the table, display side down. Brush paste evenly over the back of the sheet, including the edges.

3. Lay the back of the smaller sheet directly and squarely onto the pasted side of the first sheet.

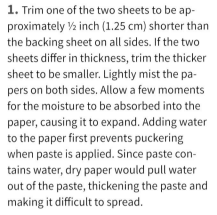

5. Carefully flip the back-coated assembly onto a smooth, hard surface, such as a piece of glass, plastic, plywood or foam-core board. Use a dry, wide brush to smooth the sheet against the board. Tap the brush end against the glued margin, all around, to ensure a good bond to board's surface. Allow to dry. Overnight is usually sufficient, depending on the humidity.

6. After the back-coated paper has dried, insert a knife through the "gateway" created in step 4.

4. Lay a strip of scrap paper across both sheets to act as a "gateway," which will allow you to easily insert a knife between the board and the paper after the glue dries.

7. Carefully release the paper from the board by sliding the knife along the pasted margin. Apply water to the adhering edges of paper and glue to clean the board for future use.

8. The released, back-coated paper is ready for trimming and wet-folding.

Cutting and Trimming Papers to Size

Making attractive jewelry requires making each piece just the right size. It can be difficult to make perfect squares. Trying to fold jewelry from paper that is not square is annoying, more difficult, and the results might look sloppy. The beads we used in our photo models were often folded from 2-inch (5.1 cm) squares, sometimes even a bit smaller. If you try to cut these squares individually, using scissors or even a paper cutter, it is too easy for the paper to move, because there is little room to hold it securely. Advancing the strip along the marked divisions on the paper cutter makes less perfect squares than inserting the paper under the blade until it contacts a jig stop (a physical stop provided by a sticky note, or some other edge). Adding pen or pencil lines can soil the paper. We like to use a paper cutter to make long strips of the folding paper, and then fold strategic creases to mark the divisions of each square across the strip where needed.

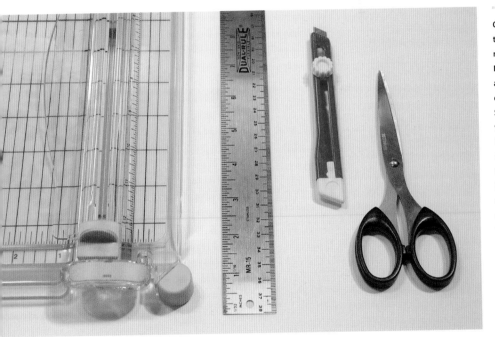

Choose the right cutting tool for the task: Paper cutter, sturdy ruler and sharp blade, scissors. Each has its own purpose. An accurate paper cutter is useful for cutting numerous small squares. Sharp scissors work fine, but if you expect to be pre-folding the basic crease patterns or grids onto larger sheets of printed washi-style papers for efficiency (and then cutting them into smaller squares after the initial creases are made), you will want a paper cutter with a firm edge for you to place selected, pre-creased valley folds against before cutting.

1. Unless you are first pre-creasing a whole sheet of paper, we suggest you start by cutting a strip of the paper at the desired width (say, 2 inches / 5.1 cm). If your paper is patterned, you should consider incorporating elements of that design, changing the width accordingly. Check to make sure the sides are parallel: Simply loop the strip of paper to align one end on top of the opposite end. If the widths at each end are equal, and the edges are straight, then the sides must be parallel. If the ends are not true, trim them while holding one on top of the other.

2. With the two ends aligned, crease the strip horizontally at its center (fold the strip in half). Your center fold is now perfectly perpendicular to the side edges.

3. Now unfold and turn the piece so the valley crease is vertical. Valley-fold the left and right halves of the bottom edge to meet at the center crease. Check the placement to make sure the two short ends are aligned, while a neat, 90-degree corner forms a "V" centered at the crease. Flatten to crease the first two diagonal folds.

4. Valley-fold the lower 90-degree corner up to align at the center crease (between the two vertical halves), and crease where the diagonals intersect the edges, forming right triangles. Install another horizontal crease where the point of the triangular flap intersects the middle vertical crease.

5. Unfold, and use the final crease as a guide to fan-fold the rest of the strip to mark perfect squares.

6. Align the strip edge along the paper cutter's grid, while placing the crease of each square's division on the cutting edge. This will allow you to make precise squares with each cut perpendicular to the strip's sides.

When cutting long, pre-creased strips, install valley folds between the squares that can be set tightly against the cutter-bar edge for precise cuts.

Choosing a Paper Trimmer

- Make sure the device is designed to securely hold the paper in place during the cutting process.

- Choose a trimmer with full safety guards that keep your fingers out of harm's way while the blade is in motion.

- Whether plastic or metal, be sure the mechanism is sturdy, sharp, and tightened so there is no play.

- Your decision will depend upon what size paper stock you will be using most often. Larger cutters are often more substantial, more durable, and expensive. Small cutters are more convenient to pack when you travel.

- Check to be sure the cutter makes perfect squares. Check this by cutting two squares, and then turn one 90 degrees to the other. If they do not perfectly align after one is rotated, then the papers are not square. If the cutter is not perfect, is it adjustable?

Tips for Using a Paper Trimmer

- Be sure the cutting blade is sharp. Sharpen or replace the blade when necessary.

- Cut one sheet at a time. It is tempting to try to save time by stacking multiple sheets on the deck, but when you are working with fancy, expensive papers, cutting one sheet at a time saves the blade, and produces the most accurate cut.

- Avoid cutting materials that can dull the blade. Dedicate a pair of inexpensive scissors, or a disposable utility knife blade, for cutting those materials.

- Use a stable workbench or table with adequate lighting that throws no shadows at the cutting edge.

- Use the guide rails and measuring marks consistently. If you are using a sliding tooth, rotary blade, or lever arm paper trimmer with a marked (gridded) layout deck, decide which part of the division mark yields the most accurate cut, and then always align your stock to that place on each division mark (right, left, or center).

- Always return the blade lock to the safe position. If you get called away, you would not want anyone else to get hurt.

Basic Tools

Unlike other forms of jewelry making, folding paper requires no torches, kilns, ovens, lathes, chisels, or glass cutters. You probably already have all the tools you need to get started. True, there are many specialized jewelry maker's tools available that can make certain tasks easier or neater.

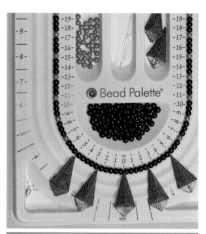

The following tools are those we use the most:

- Smooth jaw, flat-nose pliers
- Round-nose pliers (with tapered, rounded tongs)
- Plastic (nylon) jaw pliers
- Flush-cut wire cutters (often called close-nip, or "side cut")
- Tweezers
- "Bone" folding tool
- Beader's needle
- Thimble
- Crimpers
- Ruler
- Razor knife or blade
- Scissors
- Small brush for dabbing glue

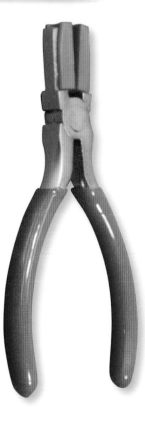

Special beader's trays or boards with length markings may help you center and arrange your necklace or bracelet elements. We find them handy to ensure that we end up with enough string or chain to complete the project after all of the elements are wrapped or secured. Of course you can make your own reference board by covering a small board or table tray with a piece of blanket, foam, or leather—any surface that will prevent round beads from rolling. Just trace your favorite necklace onto it to make a template for length comparisons, element arrangements, and adjustments.

There are several excellent technique books about making jewelry that list a host of tools and labor-saving devices. Some may not be essential to every reader, but you may find just what you need to make your favorite projects even more enjoyable.

Building Pieces of Origami Jewelry

Use gemstones and beads of metal, shell, or glass, along with basic jewelry-making tools and findings, to show off your fancy paper "jewels."

Refer to this section as needed, and soon you will become familiar enough with this material to use it creatively to design new pieces of your own. The study and practice of jewelry making is vast. There are many books that cover the subject in greater depth. It would take many volumes to represent it fairly, and so our aim is to provide you with only the essential techniques. We do make use of a small variety of easy to obtain tools and materials, but even with these limited techniques and materials, you will be able make an infinite variety of earrings, pins, and necklaces. We hope you apply our simple origami "jewels" to your future works using any of the more advanced jewelry making guides.

Above right: Inexpensive storage cases keep beads and findings ready for your next jewelry-making session.

Right: Origami jewelry does not require the expensive jewelry-making equipment and space that metal smiths and glass-blowers need! This is a professional jewelry workshop where visitors can peer through windows to watch craftspeople at work, Coral Kingdom, near Kaneohe, HI.

Below: Pre-formed eye pins, head pins, jump rings, and ear wires are inexpensive and easily available. (Of course, you could learn wire working and make all of your own!)

Findings

Fine jewelers set precious stones and beautiful gems into interesting, wearable arrangements.

You too can artistically arrange your origami elements, such as any of our beads, perhaps folded in different sizes and colors, into creative combinations and patterns by employing a variety of jewelry making materials:

- Clasps
- Pin backs
- Earring findings
- Wirework: hoops, rings, eyelets, wraps
- Cords and chains

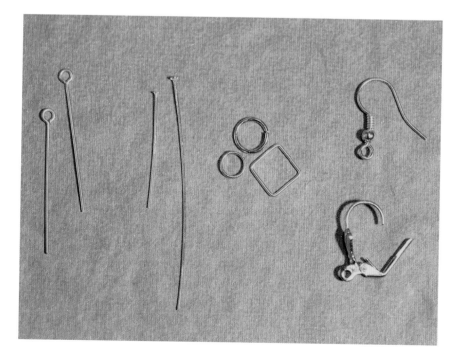

Clasps

Chains, cords of various composition, monofilament, and lengths of wire are all good choices for making necklaces and bracelets. They all need special hardware, called clasps, to join the ends for wearing around the neck or wrist. There are many from which to choose. We use four different types for the projects photographed in this book: crimps, lobster claws, barrel clasps, and magnetic.

A selection of ready-made clasp elements: crimps, lobster claws, barrel clasps, and magnetic. There are many other kinds from which to choose.

The clasps shown below are of the crimp variety. They are specially designed to accept cords, filaments, and wires. Crimps come in different sizes and types. Some have clasps attached; others have a loop for attaching a clasp. Be sure to select the size of crimp end that will accept the diameter of your stringing material.

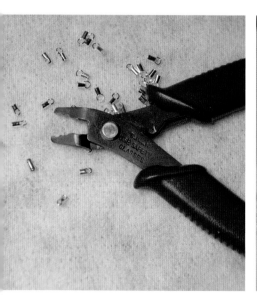

Crimp Clasp Attachment

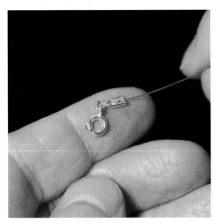

1. Insert one end of a cord or wire.

2. Crimp to secure.

3. String elements.

4. Insert the other end of the cord or wire.

5. Crimp to secure.

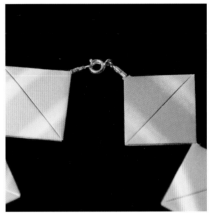

6. The completed crimp clasp attachment.

Lobster Claw Clasp Attachment

1. Open the wire loop using jeweler's pliers.

2. Slip the loop of the other piece over the open end.

3. Close the wire loop using jeweler's pliers.

4. The completed lobster claw clasp attachment.

Pin Backs

Pins are probably the most popular form of origami jewelry. They can be as simple or as elaborate as you wish. Most pin backs are made of metal, and include a hinged pin and a catch. If you simply glue your folded origami element to the shiny metal pin back bar, it might detach, and so we recommend first wrapping the attachment bar with a small piece of paper. Use enough paper to go all the way around the attachment bar and then some, and then glue not only the paper to the metal, but also the end of the paper back onto the paper, surrounding the metal attachment bar in a sleeve of paper.

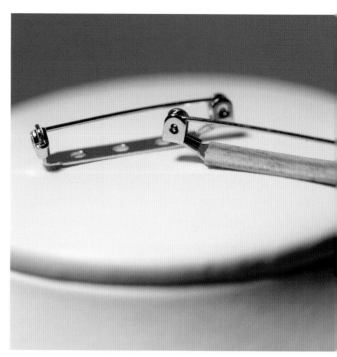

Since many popular origami designs were first developed to be viewed from only one side (for flat greeting cards or scrapbooks), those subjects work well as pins.

Some craft-shop pin backs come with a convenient cushioned adhesive strip. This works fine for temporary pieces, but an adhesive pin back applied to a piece of origami is not usually permanent. Below is a method for creating a good bond using a pin back, permanent glue and strong paper.

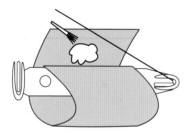

1. Cut paper to fit between the hinge and catch of a pinback. Be sure to make the strip long enough to wrap around the pinback bar at least one and a half times. Open the pin catch. Apply glue and wrap the paper around the bar of the pinback. Clean away any excess glue, close the pin, and let dry completely.

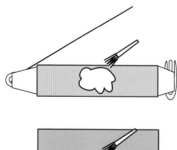

3. Cut a new piece of paper to the same width as the strip from step 1, and three times the height of the mounting bar. Apply paste to the paper and to the paper-covered mounting side of the pinback.

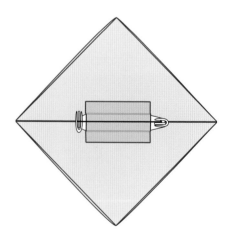

4. Apply the paste-covered mounting side of the pinback to the back of an origami brooch, then overlap the bar with the paste-covered rectangle of paper to reinforce the bond. Clean away any excess glue and let dry completely before use.

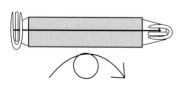

2. When dry, turn the covered pinback to the mounting side.

Ear Wires

Earrings are a charming way to wear origami art, and they make wonderful gifts. Origami earrings can complete the look of an ensemble, especially when other pieces of folded jewelry are being worn. Being small and of few elements, they are simple to make—a quick way to show off your expert craftsmanship.

The findings for earrings are readily available in many styles, but the most common are clips, and those designed for pierced ears. If you are selling or giving your earrings as a gift, consider choosing metals such as surgical steel that are labeled "hypoallergenic."

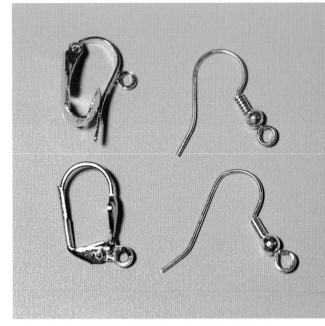

We find that earring-making is a great way to experiment with origami bead design and paper selection. You may quickly discern which combinations are successful by using only a few elements. Once you have a winning combination you may then build a matching necklace, brooch, and bracelet to complete an ensemble. Shown above is a selection of ready-made findings for pierced ears and clip-ons.

Ear Wire Attachment

1. Open the wire loop using jeweler's pliers.

2. Slip the loop of the other piece over the open end.

3. Close the wire loop using jeweler's pliers.

4. The completed earring.

Wirework

Hoops, rings, hooks, eyelets, and wraps formed of jeweler's wire are the mainstay of jewelry making.

This is collectively called "wirework," because professional jewelers often make their own findings from spools of wire. Wirework comes with its own jargon and terminology. For our purposes we shall employ only a few terms to get you started:

- **Eye pins**—one end is a split ring, forming a closed loop, the other is a pin
- **Head pins**—one end is wider, shaped like a nailhead, large enough to retain a bead
- **Jump rings**—simple split rings and special shapes used as links to connect elements
- **Ear wires**—hook-shaped loops for inserting into pierced earlobes

Although jewelers make their own findings and wire fittings, pre-formed pins, rings, and loops are now widely available, made perfectly by machine, and found in online jewelry supply houses, crafts superstores, and most larger department stores.

"Precious metals" refers to gold, silver, and platinum. Metal wires containing appreciable amounts of precious metals are much more expensive, and with the exception

of gold, can require fussy care. The most common jewelry wires and wire findings are formed of base metals: copper, nickel, iron/steel, and brass. Research and become familiar with the peculiar world of metal jewelry terminology; for example, so-called nickel-silver wire looks like silver, but surprisingly, does not contain any silver. These base metals can also be electroplated to look like other metals. These "plated" finishes can be so thin that they may rub off with wear or with cleaning in harsh chemicals. Both plated silver and sterling silver easily tarnish unless coated to prevent this. So-called "filled" wire has a thicker precious metal layer over the base metal (thicker than a "plated" product). Take care when you are working with coated and filled wires as cutters and unprotected plier jaws can sometimes easily mar them. If you are rough, it can even flake off.

Aluminum fittings are also available, but thin aluminum fittings are not strong. Steel findings of similar size are much stronger, but they will rust unless you select special grades of surgical or stainless steel. The latter two are more durable, and favored by people allergic to other metals, but since they are stronger they can be more difficult to work.

Wire comes in a wide variety of gauges (diameters) and cross-sectional shapes (round, square, triangular, or half-round—to name a few). Silver wire comes in a variety of tempers or degrees of stiffness, which can range from "dead soft" to "hard." As the wire is physically worked, even by just tapping or bending, the temper also changes (making it more stiff and brittle). Similarly, heating and then cooling it carefully softens the atomic structure of the metal in a process called annealing. Expert wire-workers use these characteristics to their advantage.

Adhesives & Glues

Let's face it: no one wants a piece of jewelry to fall apart, and so the use of glue is absolutely acceptable when making origami jewelry.

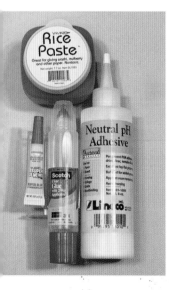

The best choice depends upon the type of paper you are using. Read the label carefully to determine its suitability, and always follow the printed usage, safety, and cleanup instructions.

Some papers are coated with plastic or other substances that may resist bonding with certain adhesives. Formulations being developed for the artist are constantly changing, so please try any adhesive first on a scrap of the paper that you want to use. Will it make the paper's colors bleed, or stain the

surrounding materials? Is it visible when dry? Keep the samples on a window sill, and then examine them after they age in the sunlight. Does the adhesive go brittle, turn yellow, or flake off?

Generally, we use polyvinyl acetate (PVA), available as an archival, water emulsion adhesive. It is strong, not water-reversible when dry, sometimes available as pH neutral, dries clear, and it does not get brittle with age. It adheres well to paper, wood, metal, some plastics, and fabric.

A Word of Caution About Intellectual Property Infringement

Accomplished folders know that most new origami designs are the intellectual property of the designers, and recognize that when the authors share their designs for non-commercial use, their art may not be used for commercial purposes without license and payment of a design royalty.

The designs diagrammed in this book are different because we know that when one folds origami jewelry, it makes no sense to purchase an expensive piece of paper to make a small corner into just one necklace, pin, or pair of earrings, and so we hereby offer all of the "jewel" designs presented in this book to the public for their unrestricted use, without obtaining any commercial use license or design royalty. PLEASE DO feel free to make several pieces of jewelry at a time! PLEASE DO fold some for your friends, or for sale on your website, at your local charity, or at a craft bazaar!

Designs such as the traditional Lily are in the public domain and are therefor fair game for your commercial use.

However, when you incorporate any of our other original and non-traditional designs (found in our many other books, DVDs, and kits) for any commercial purposes, you must first ask for, and obtain a proper written license (permission), and then pay a modest, negotiated-use royalty to Origamido, Inc. Only in this way can we be able to continue to share our designs with the public for their personal education and enjoyment.

These designs, and those like them found in our other books and kits, are the intellectual property of Origamido, Inc. Feel free to make all the jewelry you like for your personal and non-commercial gift-giving use, but please contact us at info@origamido.com before offering these items for sale, or use in any other commercial manner.

The Tuttle Story
"Books to Span the East and West"

Many people are surprised to learn that the world's leading publisher of books on Asia had humble beginnings in the tiny American state of Vermont. The company's founder, Charles E. Tuttle, belonged to a New England family steeped in publishing.

Immediately after WWII, Tuttle served in Tokyo under General Douglas MacArthur and was tasked with reviving the Japanese publishing industry. He later founded the Charles E. Tuttle Publishing Company, which thrives today as one of the world's leading independent publishers.

Though a westerner, Tuttle was hugely instrumental in bringing a knowledge of Japan and Asia to a world hungry for information about the East. By the time of his death in 1993, Tuttle had published over 6,000 books on Asian culture, history and art—a legacy honored by the Japanese emperor with the "Order of the Sacred Treasure," the highest tribute Japan can bestow upon a non-Japanese.

With a backlist of 1,500 titles, Tuttle Publishing is more active today than at any time in its past—still inspired by Charles Tuttle's core mission to publish fine books to span the East and West and provide a greater understanding of each.

Published by Tuttle Publishing, an imprint of Periplus Editions (HK) Ltd.

www.tuttlepublishing.com

Copyright © 2015 by Michael G. LaFosse and Richard L. Alexander

Library of Congress Cataloging-in-Publication Data

LaFosse, Michael G., author.
LaFosse & Alexander's origami jewelry : easy-to-make paper pendants, bracelets, necklaces and earrings / by Michael G. LaFosse and Richard L. Alexander, Origamido, Inc.
pages cm
ISBN 978-4-8053-1151-6 (paperback) -- ISBN 978-1-4629-1507-1 (ebook) 1. Origami. 2. Jewelry making. I. Alexander, Richard L., 1953- author. II. Origamido Studio. III. Title.
TT872.5.L345 2015
736'.982--dc23
2015017434

ISBN 978-4-8053-1151-6

DISTRIBUTED BY

North America, Latin America & Europe
Tuttle Publishing, 364 Innovation Drive, North Clarendon, VT 05759-9436 U.S.A.
Tel: (802) 773-8930 | Fax: (802) 773-6993; info@tuttlepublishing.com | www.tuttlepublishing.com

Japan
Tuttle Publishing, Yaekari Building, 3rd Floor, 5-4-12 Osaki, Shinagawa-ku, Tokyo 141 0032
Tel: (81) 3 5437-0171 | Fax: (81) 3 5437-0755; sales@tuttle.co.jp | www.tuttle.co.jp

Asia Pacific
Berkeley Books Pte. Ltd., 61 Tai Seng Avenue #02-12, Singapore 534167
Tel: (65) 6280-1330 | Fax: (65) 6280-6290; inquiries@periplus.com.sg | www.periplus.com

First edition
19 18 17 16 15   5 4 3 2 1   1508EP
Printed in Hong Kong

TUTTLE PUBLISHING® is a registered trademark of Tuttle Publishing, a division of Periplus Editions (HK) Ltd.